# DO WELL OR DIE

## MEMOIRS OF A WWII MOUNTAIN TROOPER

# DO WELL OR DIE

## MEMOIRS OF A WWII MOUNTAIN TROOPER

**Marty Daneman**

Brule Wisconsin

DO WELL OR DIE
Memoirs of a WWII Mountain Trooper

First Edition

Published by:
Cable Publishing
14090 E Keinenen Rd
Brule, WI 54820

Website: www.cablepublishing.com
E-mail: nan@cablepublishing.com



Soft cover: ISBN 13: 978-1-934980-86-6
ISBN 10: 1-934980-86-2

Library of Congress Control Number: 2011937188

Printed in the United States of America

## Dedicated to My One and Only

Her name was Lois Miller. She had the greatest legs of all the girls in Mr. Block's Geometry I class at Senn High School in Chicago. I couldn't help but stare...day after day after day. After about a week of that she sent word through one of her girlfriends that my staring made her nervous...would I please stop.

In a pig's eye I would. I was the designated Class Tease. By the next day I had alerted every guy in the class of the need to stare continuously at Lois' legs. They all obliged, and by the end of the class she was beet red and furious. She was dating a friend of mine at the time, and I was dating a friend of hers, who unceremoniously dumped me shortly thereafter for a more accomplished roller skater. I switched allegiances, and to the amazement of our mutual friends, I started to date Lois. It didn't take very long to fall in love. I was sixteen and she was fifteen. She still has the heart-shaped locket I gave her to mark the momentous event of our going steady.

By the time I entered the Army two years later, Lois had moved to San Francisco to be with her newly divorced mother. We embarked on an unequaled letter-writing blitz. She never missed a day. I rarely did, and she still has every letter we ever wrote to each other.

During the thirty-three months I spent in the Army, Lois became my anchor to sanity and reality. She described her everyday activities in detail so I could visualize life as if we were together all the time.

The training at Camp Hale, Colorado, and then at Camp Swift, Texas, inflicted almost unbearable physical and psychological punishment on me. Through my letters to Lois, I was able to throw off those burdens, thereby making life bearable. She gave me the strength to emotionally grow under those conditions, rather than to disintegrate.

When the 10th entered combat in Italy in early 1945, I could have recoiled under the horror and become dysfunctional. Her letters came, sometimes in bunches of five or six, to the envy of my buddies. They sustained me through the worst of it. She always understood, and never let me wallow in self-pity. I knew I had found my one and only.

# FOREWORD

I met Marty Daneman back in November 1991 when I was working on my first book, *Soldiers On Skis: A Pictorial Memoir of the 10th Mountain Division.* During my interview of him, I was impressed with his lucid and compelling way of telling a story, and I seem to recall that I told him I hoped that he would one day write his memoirs of his wartime service. Whether my encouragement had anything to do with it or not, you now hold his memoirs in your hand.

I have had the privilege of reviewing and offering my comments to the several drafts that his memoirs went through to arrive at this stage, and I can only say that Marty's writing remains as fresh and unpretentious as it did the first time I read through the initial manuscript.

There has been a plethora of books written about the 10th Mountain Division—and for good reason. The 10th was the only American division before, during, or after World War II that was specially trained for mountain and winter warfare. But, as a highly specialized division, it had to wait to be inserted into exactly the right time and place, which turned out to be the German-held northern Apennine Mountains of Italy during the last few months of 1944. Once the 10th was deployed to the combat zone, it never lost a battle or gave up an inch of ground.

The 14,000-man division was made up of a colorful cast of characters—world-class skiers and mountaineers (many of them foreign born), hotshot athletes fresh from college, a lot of guys whose IQs were pushing the upper end of the scale, and even cowboys and muleskinners (due to the fact that the division had thousands of pack mules and horses needed to carry equipment into the trackless high country). There were even a few thousand "ordinary Joes" who were part of the outfit.

I count Marty as one of the "ordinary Joes," as was my father, who was drafted into the 10th and turned into an artilleryman. Marty, by the luck of the draw, wound up in the S-2, or Intelligence, squad of his battalion in the 85th Mountain Infantry Regiment. In this book, he recounts—often with irony and dry humor, and at other times with a description of some of the horrors of combat that will bring a tear to your eye—some of his many adventures as a new ski trooper in the rarified atmosphere of the division's mountain training camp at Camp Hale, Colorado, and then in battle in Italy.

Here, along with a few thousand of his closest friends, this wiry Jewish kid from Chicago learned how to ski down snow-covered slopes, climb up rocky cliffs, and survive in harsh wilderness conditions. In short, he learned how to become a rough, tough, mountain trooper who waited with eager anticipation for the moment when he and the rest of his division would be unleashed against the Nazi foe.

On these pages the reader will encounter such flesh-and-blood characters as Johnny Dolan, Edwin "Ned" Nedoszytko, Harry Weinsaft, Tibor Mikes, Fearless Fosberg, Lieutenant James, Captain Shepard, and even Daneman's hated battalion commander, Lieutenant Colonel S. They are young men who won't soon be forgotten.

Marty has a writer's eye for fine detail and a well-tuned ear for genuine dialogue, and he leaves little to the imagination. Most of all, he captures the spirit of the time, when young men gladly lined up to serve their country, when patriotism was in full swing, when there was a war to be won, and virtually no one wanted to be left home to miss out on the great adventure.

*Do Well or Die* is his paean to his buddies who did not come home, whose names are etched forever on the long roll call known as "The Greatest Generation." And this is a great book about them.

— Flint Whitlock
Co-author, *Soldiers On Skis*

Major General George P. Hays, the 10th Mountain Division's commanding general

(U.S. Army photo)

# Prologue

In February 1945, Major General George P. Hays, Commanding General of the 10th Mountain Division, gave his first battle order. He expected a battalion of green troops, fresh from the States, to climb a sheer, ice-covered cliff in the dead of night, without artillery support, with unloaded rifles, to storm a vital German-held position we Americans called Riva Ridge, some three-and-a-half miles long and approximately 4,000 feet above sea level. Denying enemy observation from this position was the key to taking the main objective, Monte Belvedere, which would be attacked the following night. Three previous attacks by other divisions against Belvedere had failed because Riva Ridge gave perfect artillery observation to the Germans.

The colonel in charge of the daring operation objected. "This looks like a suicide mission," he told the general.

"You are supposed to be elite mountain troops," Hays responded gruffly. "You will attack. *You will do well or you will die.*"

These historic words set the theme for all future operations of the 10th Mountain Division in Italy. The division did attack and they did well. Some did die. This is the story of one soldier's participation in one of the most remarkable advances in the annals of military history.

*"This is the story of a young man caught up in the sweep of global war, training hard, doing his duty, and seeing the experience shape the course of his life. The author writes with passion, conveying the gamut of human emotions. All the while, letters to and from home provide an anchor of hope for the future. As part of the historic tapestry of the 10th Mountain Division, Do Well Or Die brings a personal wartime experience home with great power."*

– Michael Haskew, Editor, *WWII History* magazine

*"The 10th Mountain Division is one of the most unique fighting forces assembled by the United States. Equally unique are the stories of the men that made up the 10th Mountain Division. We are fortunate to have Marty Daneman's book to add to that history. He tells of the rigorous training in the Colorado Rockies and the deeply personal emotions when his friends were killed in combat in Italy. Daneman's detailed account of his experiences underscores the uniqueness of the men and the division as a whole."*

– Thomas E. Hames, Chairman, Board of Directors,
10th Mountain Division Foundation, Inc.

*"A must-read WWII story about a little-known yet elite branch of the military, the ski troops. Daneman's writing is detailed and witty; his story is powerful and humane."*

– Marcus Brotherton, author of *Shifty's War*

# Contents

# 1: Belvedere...Remembering

When he got a little itchy, carbine slung over his shoulder, its butt nestled against his hip, Captain William M. Shepard ("Shep") would amble over to my foxhole. With a sort of sheepish grin he'd say, "Daneman, do you want to take a little walk?" Then he'd stand there, broad shouldered, flat bellied, his somber, icy gaze a fitting match to the ashen pallor of his skin. Even weeks of spring skiing in the mountains that cradled Camp Hale, Colorado, and a summer of searing Texas sun at Camp Swift hadn't tinted the ghostlike mantle he wore. Parodying a character straight out of Dick Tracy, he bore the appellation, "The Ghoul." But only behind his back. You didn't play name games with your company commander.

I'd cock my head for a second like I was pondering a choice. (As if my two stripes gave me an option against his two silver bars.) Mumbling, I'd reply, "Sure." In truth, I'd have followed him to the end of the earth. His calm, no bullshit demeanor had earned my total respect. So off we'd go, not really looking for trouble, but headed for one of our outposts high in the Italian Appenines. Even during lulls in the fighting, some of our little walks led to harrowing nightmares.

The first nightmare was on a February night in 1945 on the bare saddle between Mount Belvedere and Mount Gorgolesco, somewhere north of Florence. It must have been near midnight when we started across the slopes, diligently trying to be silent. Darkness falls deeply in the Italian winter. The huge anti-aircraft spotlights ranging along peaks to our south sent their beams bouncing off the winter haze, creating the artificial moonlight by which we made our way.

Neither of us spoke. Only the rustle of our gear and the squeaky crunch of our mountain boots penetrating the frozen shell on the snow broke the silence. We stole through the trees just under the undulating crest of the tree line, wary of bypassed Krauts or their probing patrols. They still held the lower reaches north and west of the peaks, and a wrong turn would put us in their midst. With only a sidelong glance, we passed some of the anonymous dead, sprawled grotesquely, silhouetted against the snow.

Finally, beyond the ruins of a tiny mountain church, Cappel di Ronchidas, on a ridge of towering chestnut trees, we stumbled on a cluster of foxholes. Muffled voices answered our password, and whispered directions sent us further into the defense perimeter to the log-covered dugout which sheltered the 2nd Battalion's advance command post. Inside, by the flickering yellow beams of a candle, we found Lieutenant Colonel S. huddled over a map.

Suddenly the shelling, which had been intermittent, intensified.

The Germans were zeroed in on the dugout they had built and correctly surmised that we would also use. A relentless rain of shells split the earth. The ground trembled, and granules from the rent sandbags poured between the logs that formed the ceiling. The noise was painful, ear-shattering; even hands cupped over the ears could not relieve the pain of concussion.

Outside, the men who cowered in frantically dug foxholes began taking hits from overhead artillery and mortar tree-bursts. The illusionary shelter of the chestnuts instead became an umbrella of death. I worried about Johnny and Ned, my close friends who had been dispatched to an observation outpost somewhere nearby.

Some of the wounded who could still crawl headed for the dugout and soon it was crammed with men. *This isn't for me*, I thought. One lucky direct hit would have collapsed the roof and annihilated all of us. I searched for Shep, but in the sea of helmets, I couldn't pick him out. Crawling over and under the seething bodies, I slowly squeezed to the exit.

During a brief lull in the shelling, I dashed from the dugout and toward a narrow, windswept gulley outlined by a snow-covered clearing. The crescendo of crashing shell bursts persisted as I dove into the shallow trench. For what seemed like hours I pressed my face and body into the cold snow, not daring to move. Shrieking chunks of shrapnel tore through the air inches over my head, slashing huge holes in the tree trunks and sending them crashing to the ground. Nearby, pain-filled cries of "Medic" and "Mama" punctuated the screams of the wounded.

From somewhere along the ridge came a cry that ricocheted from the peaks: "*HERE THEY COME!!!*"

# 2:
# The Road to Hale is Paved with Good Intentions
# November 1942

Philip Roth hadn't even thought of *Portnoy's Complaint* when I preceded him at Chancellor Avenue School in Newark, New Jersey. I was in kindergarten there and chummed around with Abbey Fishbein, Billy Doyle, and Tony Cermele. We lived at 519 Clinton Place near the hill leading up to Summit Place. During the winter, we'd ride our sleds down that hill and were stopped by ashes spread by our fathers. In the summer, we rode makeshift wagons at breakneck speeds to the hill's bottom. Other fun was provided by memberships on football or softball teams organized as the Panther Athletic Clubs. We proudly sported our PAC sweaters.

Our interest in girls started when we were about thirteen and was fueled in part by a good set of boobs clearly visible on Elaine G., who lived atop Summit Place. The romance my brother Jerry and I got involved in, though, was between two of our teachers. We were designated the romantic-letter carriers for Mr. Jacobs and another teacher, who later wed.

Shortly after my Bar Mitzvah in 1938, my father was promoted and we moved to Chicago and an apartment at 1451 Elmdale Avenue near Senn High School. I finished eighth grade at Hayt Elementary School and was befriended by several Jewish boys. We all started high school together at Senn.

During my sophomore year I was handed an early lesson in politics. Without my knowledge, someone entered my name as a candidate for Marshall Judge—the job of assessing penalties for minor transgressions. The two prettiest girls in our class were also nominated. They each drew thirty percent of the vote while I received the remaining forty percent, and victory!

That was about the time I met Lois....

Here I am at age 13 (left) with my father Arthur and brother Jerry, photographed at a Lake Michigan beach in Chicago, circa 1938.

(Courtesy of the author)

MY ORIGINAL GOAL in life was to become a pilot. I was nuts about the Wild Blue Yonder long before the song was ever written. As a sickly, eight-year-old kid, I used to while away the time in bed creating entire fleets of World War I fighter planes out of my mother's clothespins. I couldn't wait to be old enough to join the Air Corps. The onset of World War II brought the opportunity more quickly than I had ever expected.

In 1942, when I was a seventeen-year-old senior at Senn, I heard about a new pre-enlistment program offered by the Army Air Corps. I could take a battery of tests and be in the Enlisted Reserve. I would then be called to active duty after I graduated.

I typed the application on the family's Underwood typewriter and sent it off with a three-cent stamp. It seemed the Air Corps was just as eager to have me as I was to join up, responding almost immediately was that I was accepted for testing.

The afternoon before my appointment, I presented myself at Chanute Field, about 130 miles south of Chicago. I wanted to be all set for my tests scheduled for early the next morning. The MP at the gate looked at my application with a skeptical eye and left me to figure out where I would eat and sleep that night. Just then, an officer with a spiffy uniform and shiny wings on his chest drove up to the gate. I explained my problem to him and without hesitation, he invited me to his home on the base for dinner and to spend the night in his spare bedroom. Sheer heaven! I was really impressed with the Air Corps.

I spent a restless night, but the next day found me seated in a classroom with a group of other young kids, taking some sort of IQ test, which took a matter of a couple of hours. I slogged through the easy parts but felt overwhelmed by the math section. After lunch in the mess hall, we returned to hear the verdict. I had made the cut along with a few others and was then herded into another building to begin the physical tests.

The first test was the all-important eye exam. I felt overjoyed to discover that I had perfect 20/20 vision and perfect depth perception. Next came the Japanese "Bubble Chart." If you had normal color perception, the bubbles would line up to form a particular numeral. If you had a problem (misnamed color blindness), you would see a different number, or none at all.

I saw all the colors…but the wrong ones! The officer in charge told me I was blue-green color blind. He let me take the test again, but the result didn't change. "In map reading," he explained, "you would confuse a lake and a prairie field and make a very wet emergency landing." So much for the Wild Blue Yonder. I felt heartbroken and made my way disconsolately home.

That brings me to the episode with Dave Levy. In 1942, my father was the branch manager of a house-to-house sales company. The product sold was supposed to be books, but in reality what the company sold was an easy payment plan: One dollar down and one dollar a week by mail. Dave Levy was the shipping clerk for the company, making a then-typical weekly wage of fifteen dollars.

Somehow, he managed to save enough to take a year off and attend the University of Wisconsin at Madison. Astonishingly, he showed up at the office late in 1942 wearing an Army dress uniform!

"I'm in the ski troops," he announced. Dave proceeded to tell me about learning to ski at Madison and how the draft caught up with him. He was now stationed at Camp Hale, Colorado, having a wonderful time skiing every day. I recently had seen a newsreel about that outfit and felt intrigued. Dave told me how the National Ski Patrol was recruiting men even before they were inducted into the Army.

I was hooked. Skiing had to be the next best thing to flying. All my friends were going into service at that time and I thought this would be a much better deal than that of a regular soldier crawling through the snake-and-bug-infested jungles of the South Pacific. Soon, I sent off an application.

At this point, the war was not going especially well for America and our allies. The Japanese were kicking our butts in the Pacific and German submarines, or U-boats, were sinking ships in the Atlantic faster than we could build new ones. The fledgling American Army had finally gotten into the game against the Germans, Italians, and Vichy French in North Africa, but we were getting our lunch handed to us. It wasn't until General George S. Patton took charge of American forces in North Africa that we finally started to put up a respectable showing against the enemy.

Late 1942 and early 1943 was also a time when almost every able-bodied young American male wanted to be in the armed forces—whether it be the Army, Navy, Marine Corps, or Air Force. Marching off to war was the "cool" thing to do, not to mention that we all felt it was essential for our country's—and the free world's—survival. Guys who were 4-F (physically, mentally, or morally unfit to be in the service) or were simply shirking and trying to avoid the draft were looked down upon as cowards, malingerers, or outright unpatriotic. The fact that there was an Army unit whose main job was to ski and climb mountains made the prospect of getting into such an elite unit that much more appealing.

The requirements were simple enough. You had to be a skier, an athlete, or an outdoorsman. In spite of my pack-a-day cigarette habit, I was on the Senn High track team, running the 440 and the one-mile races. I had been a weightlifter since I was fifteen, so I was wiry and strong. I would need three letters of recommendation attesting to my physical prowess and my sterling character. My coaches provided the former. A lawyer friend of my father produced the latter. Ironically, as it later turned out, he had made his fortune by representing the Chicago Mafia.

In late February 1943, I received a penny postcard from the National Ski Patrol, announcing my acceptance. It instructed me to show up at the induction center and I would automatically be sent to Camp Hale to start skiing with Dave. I had never seen a ski in my life, but with teenage exuberance, I didn't regard that as an obstacle. I counted the days until my eighteenth birthday. I knew I'd have no trouble with the physical or IQ tests, but I worried about that darn bubble chart. Would the ski troops care if I couldn't distinguish between blue and green?

On my March 9th birthday, I volunteered for induction and was directed to report for the tests a week later. When I had run the whole gamut of tests, including the slightly different set of bubble charts, I was marched past a row of recruitment officers seated behind desks. Each one was there to entice me into joining his branch of the service. It was like a job fair with limited choices.

First, I checked with the Marines. The sergeant looked over my test scores and invited me to join. I asked him about the color blindness and was astonished to learn that according to the test I had just taken, my color perception was normal. I showed him my postcard from the National Ski Patrol. He shrugged his shoulders and waved me on. I paused at the Air Corps desk with a little yearning still in my heart. The sergeant explained that the Air Cadet program was closed, but I could try for Ground Officers OCS. No thanks. I flashed my postcard at the Army desk, and the sergeant there knew exactly what to do. I soon had my orders cut to report to Camp Hale after a brief stint of induction procedures at Camp Grant, Illinois, just west of Chicago.

So it was a conversation with a shipping clerk and a fluke in an eye test that propelled me into the most memorable adventure of my life. My father glowed with pride and my mother wept when I told them of my new status as Private Martin L. Daneman, Army Serial Number 36745423, with instructions to report for duty the following week. They had already bought the little flag with the service star that announced our family had provided a member to serve his country and proudly hung it in the window. My brother, then only sixteen, was not too impressed—at least openly—but when I left for camp, he embraced me warmly.

The news was also worthy of a costly long distance phone call to my steady girlfriend, Lois, then living in San Francisco. I promised to send her my military address as soon as I had one, and we exchanged promises to write daily reports of our doings. I was among the last of my friends to enter service, so a raucous farewell party was not in the cards. A few nights before my departure my parents, my brother, and I spent a farewell evening at the 5100 Club in Chicago being entertained by a rising young comedian named Danny Thomas.

I reported back to the draft board a week after I took the oath of allegiance "to the United States of America and to the Republic…." Head held high, body proudly erect, arms swinging in military style, I marched down Elmdale Avenue. Soon I would be dispatched to Camp Grant. Then it dawned on me that my decision to volunteer was irretrievable. I would be expected to accept responsibility for all my own actions. Dad would no longer be available to bail me out of a bad decision, or advise me how to avoid making one. In short, I suddenly had passed into manhood.

As instructed, besides a little leather folder with stationery and a new Parker pen, I carried only a toilet kit—a new Dopp kit presented as a farewell gift from my family and friends. It held a brand-new bar of Lifebuoy soap in a metal container, a tube of Pepsodent toothpaste, a plastic slip-over container for my toothbrush, a new chrome Gillette safety razor with a pack of two-edged blades, and a jar of Burma Shave. Also included was a manicure kit with a nail file, scissors, and a cuticle stick. These items were intended to be the only remnants of civilian life permitted by the Army. Everything else would be shipped home.

At the draft board, a couple dozen inductees milled around, waiting for someone to take charge. My father appeared, beaming and ebullient, and took us all to a corner drug store where he treated everyone to a cup of coffee. "Can't hurt to be nice to your buddies and get you off to a good start," he whispered. The fact was that, once at Camp Grant, I never saw any of them again.

Back at the draft board, an official designated one of the inductees to be in charge and dispatched our group by streetcar to the LaSalle Street rail station. From there we joined a hoard of other new GIs and boarded trains for Camp Grant. By noon we were at the camp, marching in a rag-tag formation en route to our first barracks home. Along the road we were greeted by hoots and hollers from men in baggy fatigues, shorn of hair, heavily engaged in searching for trash. They were the "veterans," having been in the Army for as long as two to three days.

Mundane events occupied the next few days. The first cafeteria-style meal convinced me I would starve to death long before an enemy bullet found its mark. Gobs of nauseating, fat-ringed pork were heaped on my plate, but ended up in the huge garbage cans at the mess hall's exit. I managed to stave off hunger with mashed potatoes and slabs of bread. The rest of the afternoon was spent waiting in line for a one-minute session in a barber's chair, whereupon all remaining shreds of individual dignity were shorn with my hair.

Then we were led to the slaughterhouse, where rank amateur medics-in-training punctured our arms with horse-sized needles containing mysterious liquids, designed to cause fainting spells, but supposedly meant to prevent disease. Then back to the barracks for a brief bull session to speculate on tomorrow's fate. I took the time to relate the day's adventures to Lois using my newly granted privilege of free postage. Instead of licking and affixing a stamp, all I needed to do was write my name and newly memorized serial number on the upper right corner of the envelope.

On the morrow, after a fast breakfast composed of greasy bacon, runny eggs, and burned toast, we were led to a huge, school-room-type edifice. Therein we took the infamous IQ and aptitude tests, which settled the final destinations of many. Those with high grades had a shot at a specialized school. Those with "grunt grades" were meant for infantry replacement camps. I managed an adequate 110 score and was tempted with an offer to go to radio school. But I was already bound for the ski troops and stuck to my guns.

Haberdashery day was next. We lined up in a cavernous warehouse and proceeded to move auto-assembly-line fashion from one counter to the next. We were measured for underwear, shirts, pants, socks, shoes, and jackets. Items approximating our size were thrust into our waiting arms and then crammed into barracks bags. We were marched back to the barracks to try on everything. Afterward, we put on the fatigue uniform, complete with the laced-up canvas leggings, a real mystery to solve. We packed our civilian duds for shipment home. Spare time was spent "policing" the area, looking for wayward cigarette butts. We joined in the hazing of new arrivals. After all, *we* were now the "veteran" inductees.

Big surprise! Friday afternoon we were awarded weekend passes. There was a mad rush for the Illinois Central depot and a place to stand in the jammed, ancient cars. I found one on the platform between cars, where I was the target for every piece of soot and steam the locomotive could toss my way. Back in Chicago, after a call to let Mom know I'd be home for a late dinner, I caught the northbound El (elevated train) as it circled the Loop (GIs rode for free) and headed back home feeling pretty spiffy in my insignia-less uniform. I spent the weekend showing it off for my few still-civilian buddies and their "steadies." It would have been nice to see Lois, but she was 1,500 miles away in California.

Sunday night I boarded the train and returned to Camp Grant. At roll call Monday morning, two of us were called out and sent to the orderly room. There we were informed we had been assigned to Camp Hale, Colorado, and would depart immediately. The route would take us back to Chicago, then overnight via the *Denver Rocket* to Colorado. After a day's layover, we would catch the Denver & Rio Grande Railroad, which would take a full day to circle down through the Royal Gorge, back to Leadville, thence to Pando, Colorado, which was the railroad's name for the Camp Hale depot. The other new ski trooper, whose name is lost in memory, was in his mid-twenties. Based on his assumed greater maturity, he became my leader. We made the train connections in Chicago (with time for a quick call to my dad to tell him I was on my way), and we boarded the *Rocket*. We spent the entire trip in the Bar Car being feted by the "feather merchants" (guilt-ridden civilians) who were using the train for commercial travel. No one questioned my age when I asked for a rum and Coke. When we arrived in Denver, we headed for the USO to kill time until our Camp Hale overnight train was due to depart. There we learned we could substitute a four-hour bus ride tomorrow for our overnight train ride beginning today and thus get to spend a full day and night in Denver. "No soap," my companion decided. He had the IQ and inflexibility of a mule and couldn't understand that our orders called for arrival the next night, which the bus could accomplish by leaving in the morning instead of tonight. So we went by train.

As it turned out, the train was overbooked, and we were given folding bridge chairs upon which to spend the night. That was not for me. I wandered from the coach into a more deluxe car and struck up a conversation with a family en route to Salt Lake City. I was invited to join them and settled into an unoccupied chair adjacent to theirs. The conductor attempted to order me out of the car, but the kindly family protested loudly, and I was permitted to stay there for the remainder of the trip. To top it off, in the morning they bought me breakfast and saved the government the value of a coupon I could have used. There is some justice in the world. My traveling companion spent the night scrunched up in his bridge chair.

My first glimpse of Camp Hale came as the Denver & Rio Grande descended the long, steep grade from Tennessee Pass, a hundred miles west of Denver. Mountain peaks rose on all sides of a narrow valley. Hundreds of white, two-story barracks covered the flat valley floor that was bisected by a channeled mountain stream. That monotony was relieved by a scattering of Western movie-style corrals, each of which held a coterie of huge Missouri mules. Scattered about were single-storied buildings that housed headquarters of various units, movie theaters, and an oversized service club. A long string of connected buildings at the valley's northern end housed the post hospital.

A view of the southern half of Camp Hale that filled Colorado's Pando Valley, between Minturn and Leadville

(U.S. Army photo)

We arrived at Pando shortly after daybreak. It appeared to be an abandoned depot. An MP wandered by in a jeep. After he inspected our papers, we were ordered to shoulder the barracks bags and carry them to the Camp Hale gate a hundred or so yards away. I thought I was in pretty good shape, but thanks to the oxygen-depleted, 9,000-foot altitude, that illusion disappeared between the depot and the gate. Half staggering, I approached the guarded entrance. Once there, I was told to report to the headquarters building a half-mile farther on. It took the better part of half an hour to go that distance as the thin air left me breathless and exhausted. My two-pack-a-day habit didn't help, either. My tobacco consumption had doubled since my induction.

A clerk examined my papers and assigned me to Headquarters Company Triple Prime (later Headquarters, 3rd Battalion)* of the 86th Mountain Infantry Regiment, 10th Light Division (Alpine, Pack), and gave me a barracks number. More staggering, more exhaustion, more panting and puffing, but at last I dragged myself into my new home, where half a dozen other young men lounged lazily on their steel, double-deck bunks. At last, I really was in the ski troops.

* A battalion was approximately 1,000 men.

# 3: My Crock Runneth Over

We were allowed to loaf for a couple of days due to the mountaineering doctrine called "acclimation." Simply put, it took several days for a body to adjust to the high altitude at Camp Hale. We were indoctrinated by Army Mountain Theory Number One: "It is possible by diligent, persistent, and constant application of devotion to task to rid the Rocky Mountains of every rock and pebble in sight." We spent hours policing (read "picking up") hundreds of thousands of stones ranging from microscopic to boulder size from the areas surrounding our barracks. We gathered them into huge piles that later were loaded into trucks and deposited at some unknown location. Those stones had been dumped there to convert a mountain swamp into level ground for the camp. The supply was inexhaustible.

The theory of basic training was to destroy by means of tyrannical discipline any remaining sense of individuality we had. Our total subjugation to the whims of authority was quickly made crystal clear. For example, after each day's training, we made a mad dash into the barracks, discarded our fatigues, and cleaned up. Those who had any resemblance of a beard re-shaved to appear glossy-faced. We changed into our "Class A" uniforms, and our new combat boots with the fuzzy, unshineable finish, were checked for any dust or dirt.

Every speck of dust and dirt was also lovingly removed from our weapons, which may have spent the day being dragged through the mud on a rainy summer day. The initial training weapon was a 1903 A3 Springfield bolt action .30-caliber rifle, circa World War I. The newer M-1 Garand semi-automatic rifle was not yet available in sufficient quantities to be wasted on mere recruits. The cleaning tools were toothbrushes, shaving brushes, and cotton gun patches soaked in gun oil and drawn through the barrel on a string.

We then lined up for an inspection that we were pre-ordained to fail. This meant after-hours additional duty (policing the grounds). Worst of all, a failed inspection meant no weekend pass.

While standing in the ranks awaiting inspection, we were at rigid attention, with rifle butt alongside the right foot. When the inspecting officer approached, we brought it smartly to "port arms," diagonally across our chests. We brought the bolt to the rear by pulling the operating handle crisply up and to the right with our right hand. The officer would then grab the rifle and go through the charade of looking for dust or grease, which he inevitably found, and issued a "gig." With endless practice and effort, I learned to have my rifle exquisitely clean, but when standing at attention awaiting inspection, the butt of the rifle rested on the ground adjacent to my foot. The comment and gig for "dusty butt plate" that followed meant that you had done an excellent job but were nevertheless to be penalized. I soon learned to put a small pebble next to my right foot while awaiting inspection, upon which I rested the rifle butt. Robbed of the usual punishable offense, I remember one inventive officer gigging me for dust on my shoe soles.

When enough new bodies had arrived at Camp Hale to fill out the company roster (a company was about 200 men), the task of giving us soldierly skills began. Days began before dawn as we filed into nearby open spaces and lined up to go through tortuous calisthenics. The most sadistic of all was the infamous Burpee, a devil's concoction which included squats, leg thrusts, push-ups, and stand-ups…all in one continuous motion. We spent hours, days, and weeks going through the prescribed curriculum of learning close-order drill, military courtesy, rifle handling, dry-firing marksmanship, bayoneting, gas-mask donning, care and cleaning of and use of every piece of equipment issued, primitive map reading, conditioning hikes that gradually lengthened to twenty miles, and finally, firing a newly issued real M-1 Garand rifle with real bullets at real targets.

In typical Army fashion, we were dispatched to the firing range for qualification in the midst of a freak summer snowstorm. In a situation that limited visibility to one hundred yards, we were required to fire at targets five hundred yards away. Needless to say, the entire company flunked the firing test, having wasted hundreds of rounds of ammunition. We took the test again a few weeks later, and nearly everyone qualified as at least a "Marksman." Those who didn't qualify were retrained and retrained until they did. I made "Sharpshooter," having barely missed a score high enough for "Expert." I did fine until the "Rapid Fire," during which I fired so rapidly that the recoil pulled the rifle from the necessary aiming point.

The camp had a "fun-firing" indoor range that accommodated .22 caliber firing. There I qualified for Expert on the .22 and the .45 pistol, but it didn't really count for anything.

Beginning day one at Camp Hale and all the way through basic training, I became close with an Irish kid from Cliffside Park, New Jersey, named Johnny Dolan. We had the same offbeat sense of humor and resigned acceptance of the bullshit that inundated us during basic training. We grinned at each other over the hyperbole that was spun about the boastful love affairs by some of the men, not believing a word of it.

I took the upper of the two-story bunk beds; Johnny claimed the lower bunk. Johnny and I sat together for every meal, shared food packages our families sent, and spent long hours in deep discussions. We became closer than brothers. At the end of basic, I reserved space at the guesthouse for my mom and dad, who were scheduled to come for a short visit. Unfortunately, I came down with pneumonia the day before they were to arrive, and their entire visit with me took place at the base hospital. I got word to Dave Levy about their visit, and he and Johnny managed to show them around the post.

When I recovered and reported back to Headquarters Triple Prime, 86th Mountain Infantry, I discovered that a new regiment (about 3,000 men) had been formed—the 85th. I was now a member of Headquarters Company, 2nd Battalion, of that regiment. Many of my close friends, including Johnny, had been transferred to the same company and dispersed into one or another of the specialty platoons of Headquarters Company. The next phase of training was to begin immediately.

My S-2 (combat intelligence) squad at Camp Hale: Front row (L-R) Bob Lucas, Tibor Mikes, me. Back row: Johnny Dolan, Wally Barron, Bert Hirtle, Joe Carr.

(Author photo)

With my body severely weakened by ailing lungs, by inexorable Army logic I was assigned to an 81mm mortar squad with the unenviable job of lugging around a forty-five-pound baseplate in addition to my ninety-pound rucksack of life-saving equipment. Johnny, impaired by faulty vision barely corrected by thick, Army-issue lenses, was to be in the S-2 Recon squad, where good vision was an absolute requirement. I was not a happy camper.

The mortar, which lobs a deadly finned missile, consists of four parts, each carried by one man. The gunner carries a light-weight sighting device which attaches to the tube through which the round is fired. The tube leans on a bipod and rests on the baseplate, which is designed to absorb the recoil of discharge. Each of the latter parts weighs better than forty pounds. I came out of the hospital so weak I could hardly stand, but my absence while in the hospital guaranteed my assignment to that job.

Worst of all, I would never get to ski. Instead, I would be equipped with snowshoes because of the extra weight. I barely made it up the hill to the Pearl Creek mortar range on our first training mission. I complained bitterly to Johnny about his plush assignment versus my grunt job, and he began to lobby incessantly to get me into his outfit. When one of his squad was transferred to regimental headquarters, Johnny convinced Lieutenant "Jessie" James, the intelligence officer, to interview me as a potential replacement. With obvious misgivings, Lieutenant James let me join what sounded like the elite squad of the battalion. The word "intelligence" sounded much better than "mortar," and instead of my rucksack and a forty-five-pound baseplate, I would lug a rifle, my pack, and a pair of binoculars. More importantly, I would ski.

Later in the summer of 1943, while American and British troops were overrunning the island of Sicily and pushing the Germans and Italians back to the mainland of Italy, we were running a series of CP (command post) problems at Hale. The planning, reconnaissance, communications, and supply sections of battalion headquarters spent a few days in the field directing the operations of the battalion, whose line companies were training elsewhere or practicing squad and platoon maneuvers. The S-2 squad had little to do with those kinds of maneuvers, but the new S-2 sergeant, Tibor Mikes, used the time wisely to polish our skills on map reading, observation, and stealthy movement through all kinds of terrain and conditions.

By fall, we could move undetected, day or night, to almost any spot on the map, make our observations about enemy dispositions, take a prisoner of war, and get back to HQ none the worse for wear. Our proficiency was further honed by classes in the skills that other infantry specialties required. We could load, aim, and fire every weapon allotted the division—pistols, rifles, submachine guns, bazookas, mortars, 37mm antitank guns and 75mm pack guns—as the need arose. We learned to use every radio, lay and connect communications wire, and handle every medical emergency except brain surgery.

I spent a week at "mule-packing" school learning just how obstreperous a tired mule could be. I learned how to tie a bundle of supplies to the back of one of those critters in a way that couldn't be bucked off. I even learned not to turn my back on them lest I get a fierce nip on the butt or a well-placed kick. A week or two of handling guard dogs completed the animal phase of my training. Mountaineering skills were next on the agenda.

## 4:
## On Belay

"On belay!" Johnny hollered through cupped hands, although he stood only a few feet from me, perched on a narrow ledge of granite a few hundred feet above the valley floor. That meant we were tied together with a nylon rope around our waists and positioned so that, with one of us climbing, the other would be ready to protect the other in case of a fall. Below us, Homestake Creek trickled toward its junction with the undulating rapids of the Eagle River, a few miles downstream.

"On belay!" I half-jokingly screamed to emphasize that I got the message.

"Climbing," came the automatic response. His Hibernian, square-jawed face was framed by his helmet liner. Piercing gray-blue eyes squinted through silver-framed GI spectacles, which he had meticulously cleaned with spit and a gangrenous handkerchief a few minutes before. The glasses could never camouflage the crinkles that radiated from the corners of his eyes. That's how you read Johnny: by the corners of his eyes, and the set of his jaw. The rest of his face was a carefully studied blank, except when the joke of the moment cracked him up. When that happened his smile spread from ear to ear. His most vicious comment of disapproval would be a hissed, "Jheez," through tightly clenched teeth and barely parted lips.

As he turned toward the cliff that rose to an overhang above him, the slightly rounded shoulders gave an illusion of bulk to his body that wasn't really there. He was lean and hard after four months of tortured training at Camp Hale.

I sat on a small flat spot on the ledge, straddling the twelve-inch stump of a pine tree. The heels of my rubber-studded mountain boots were firmly planted against small ridges that appeared as wrinkles in the rock. One hundred twenty feet of olive-drab 7/16 nylon rope stretched between us. The running end, tied to Johnny, ran through my right hand, across my lower back, and through my left hand, then fell in a graceful loop over the cliff edge toward the valley floor, and back up to the loop knotted around my waist. The principle of "belay" is that, should Johnny fall, the friction of the rope around me would act as a brake. My firm position against the rock would limit the distance of his fall to twice his height above me.

This was to be our final test of mountaineering. The weeks we had spent bivouacked in the meadow bordering Homestake Creek below had begun with endless hours of knot-tying practice. Then came the gamut of scrambling over scree and talus slopes, free climbing over low cliffs and up narrow chimneys, and rappelling fifty feet over the edge of an overhanging rock. We learned to listen for the

Who says city boys can't climb mountains? Here I am doing a "free climb" up a Colorado cliff.

(Author photo)

ascending scale of ringing "clangs" when hammering pitons into minute cracks in the rocks. The sound told us that we had hammered it in securely. Then followed days of climbing, roped in pairs or threes, rigging and riding aerial tramways, and climbing impossible routes with foot-slings on an angling rope until our self-confidence was supreme.

Johnny, with the cockiness of the Irish, considered himself the better athlete and appointed himself lead climber. He studied the crags above him like a chess player as he planned a series of moves that would carry him to "victory." "Move only one limb at a time" had been drummed into us throughout the training. Johnny carefully observed the protocol by keeping the other three in place every time he moved to a new position. In a few minutes he had found enough nubs in the rock to hold the slender edge of a boot, or narrow cracks into which he could jam a few fingers or a fist, so that he now stood precariously spread-eagled just below a low overhang, about thirty feet above me. The rope hung through the air from my gloved right hand to his waist with just enough slack to exert no pull, but direct enough to shorten a fall should he slip.

"Back off!" I yelled. "The overhang's too big."

"I can't see my feet," came the response. "I'll have to go over it."

One hand, then the other, reached over the rounded top of the overhang, and clutched frantically in vain for unseen crevices or handholds. Suddenly, his left foot slipped off its narrow perch. Held only by his body's friction on the rock, he began to slide precipitously toward the canyon floor, one hundred feet below. He looked over at me, face perfectly blank, no consternation, no fear, totally devoid of expression, and said in a conversational tone, "I'm going."

Now it was *my* problem, and I had practiced this only a dozen or so times. I had to wrap the "downhill" end of the rope against my waist to provide friction for the "brake," and dig my heels into the rock to prevent being pulled off the cliff when Johnny's 160 pounds came to a shuddering halt at the end of the rope. I had played out only thirty or so feet of rope when he fell, and if everything held, he would end up dangling well above the jagged rocks on the canyon floor after falling no more than sixty feet. That's as high as a six-story building!

But which hand was "downhill?" With no time to think it out, I threw both hands around my waist, dug in my heels, wrapped my knees tighter around the stump, and closed my eyes. The shock felt like I had been hit by a tank. I opened my eyes to find myself staring up at the sky. Both hands still held the rope, and they were crossed around my waist. But I was hanging upside-down over the edge of the cliff, held only by my legs, which were scissored around the tree stump. For a numbing moment I hung there, disoriented, legs trembling with the effort to hang on. The rope swung in gentle arcs below me as Johnny's body acted like a massive pendulum.

"Johnny!" I hollered. "Johnny, are you okay?"

No answer. Just the inexorable, almost unbearable force of his weight trying to tear the rope from my hands, or pull my body over the edge to join him.

"*Medic!*" I screamed.

Other GIs began to form upside-down images on nearby crags.

"Hang on." "Hold 'em." "We're coming," came the chorus. I was in a cold sweat, trembling with fatigue, my arms and legs screaming for relief. I felt a stirring on the end of the rope, then the weight disappeared as the rope went slack. I heard Johnny yell, "Climbing."

Soon our rock-climbing instructor was towering over me. He grabbed me by the shirt and hauled me upright. "On belay," he shouted to Johnny as he wrapped the coil of rope around his shoulder in a standing belay. I sat on the narrow cliff, shuddering with relief as Johnny's bare head rose above the ledge, shepherded by another instructor, carrying the helmet liner that had ricocheted to the canyon floor. He had reached Johnny from below and pulled him, dazed with the wind knocked out of him, to the safety of a narrow cleft. Like the apocryphal cure for falling off a horse, the instructor had ordered, "Get your ass up that cliff."

We were off the cliffs thirty minutes later, shuffling along the trail that led to the little mountain meadow where our tents were lined up like tract housing. Johnny turned to me, threw an arm over my shoulder, and with the little crinkled lines around his eyes a dead giveaway, said, "Daneman, you asshole, you broke my glasses."

# 5: The White Stuff

The first real snow came to the Pando Valley in late October of 1943. Not the salt-and-pepper type of ground cover that had come and gone several times since Labor Day, nor the freak blizzard that had buried us for a few hours that midsummer day on the rifle range. This snowfall began on Saturday afternoon and by Sunday morning, a solid four-inch blanket hid the ugliness of the barren valley floor. The stone rubble bulldozed to form platforms for the posts that supported the military buildings would not be visible again until the spring thaw. On Sunday morning, while most of the men slept off the exhaustion of the week's training, I put on skis for the first time.

Yes, I had the prerequisite three letters of recommendation to qualify as a ski trooper, but they spoke to my prowess as an athlete on the track, not as a mountain man. The truth was I never had seen a pair of skis up close, much less *schussed* a mountain.

The skis were a towering seven feet long, designed to help the skier carry back-breaking loads through deep powder snow. Layers of laminated hickory were edged by narrow metal strips to give the illusion of control on icy surfaces. The aluminum bindings were wedge-shaped at the toe, permitting the extra-wide toes of the mountain boot to slide into place. A steel cable looped from an adjustable mounting in front of the boot to a coiled spring at the heel. An impossible-to-handle lever locked everything into place.

After rubbing a thin coating of wax from a cardboard tube onto the boards, I carried the contraption to an adjacent field. I slipped my boots into the toe plates, wedged my heels into the coils at the cable ends, stood up, and promptly landed on my ass. I dragged myself up on the bamboo poles and—after a few more pratfalls—began to take a few tentative steps. Within an hour I was making good progress, slipping and sliding along the valley floor, but able to stay upright. Formal ski training began that week.

B Slope was a gentle rise that began at 9,300 feet, just beyond the bayonet course at the south end of Camp Hale. It ultimately rose through heavy pine and aspen timber to become the nearly 12,000-foot Taylor Hill. Here we were to learn the basics of military skiing before progressing to more sophisticated techniques at Cooper Hill, which sat astride the Continental Divide, seven miles to the south. First came cross-country level skiing, which we diligently practiced every morning. Then came climbing, which progressed rapidly from easy traversing with a step-turn or kick-turn at the end of each track's leg to tedious sidestepping on steeper pitches. The final technique to learn was the exhausting herringbone, which left our arms and shoulders numb with fatigue.

The note on the back of this snapshot says, "Me again, on my way to a good spill—and I did, too!" Taken at our main training hill at Cooper Hill, a few miles south of Camp Hale, December 1943.

(Courtesy of the author)

Learning downhill techniques was much more fun, beginning with the snowplow, then the stem turn, and finally an unofficial Arlberg which worked well in deep snow under heavy loads, for which the Christie was completely the antithesis. When we could, we'd sneak a few in anyway. (If you want to learn any of those techniques, find yourself a good instructor.)

The move to Cooper Hill was our first experience in cold-weather camping, and that required a march with full ninety-pound field packs from the camp to the 10,275-foot summit of Tennessee Pass. Johnny and I, as battalion scouts, led the march up Highway 24. Our main job was slowing down the rare automobile or truck that came roaring down from the pass so they would not endanger the long lines of marching troops. Carrying our full packs, with skis arranged in an "A" frame and attached to our rucksacks, still permitted us to carry our intimidating rifles, so we had little resistance when we waved down the traffic and asked them to slow down.

The only buildings at the base of Cooper Hill were an aid station, a headquarters building (to give officers shelter in bad weather), and a mess hall. Meals were served cafeteria-style with the food dumped into mess kits, which we precariously balanced as we walked out to bivouac areas. We ate while seated on stumps or logs, leftovers from some timber-harvesting era. Farther up the hill, a tarpaper shack housed the power generator for a mile-long T-bar, then the longest ski tow in the country.

Our two-man mountain tents were deluxe accommodations compared with the shelter halves "pup tents" used by regular infantry. Made of waterproof nylon, they had a sewn-in floor, a tunnel entrance and ventilator tubes at each end. The tubes were supposed to prevent the accumulation of moisture from our breath as we slept, but they never accomplished their intended function. Invariably, in above-freezing weather, we awoke with our sleeping bags in puddles. When colder temperatures prevailed, the inside of the tent was covered with a layer of ice that we tried to pick off and throw out of the tent. The tents were reversible—white on one side for camouflage in winter, and olive drab on the other to match summer's palette. Temperatures usually dropped well below freezing at night. Survival required that we learned a few tricks from the mountaineers among us.

We no longer relied only on hip pads and our double down-filled sleeping bags. We learned the advantage of a six- or eight-inch-thick bough foundation for the tent. These were constructed by laboriously collecting (illegally and to the consternation of all foresters) pine branch tips that were layered at an angle to form a resilient mattress. A reflector of slant-stacked logs directed heat from our campfires into the tent. A single candle mounted in an empty C-ration can provided light for letter writing. This completed our luxurious quarters.

Every night was party time. In a small clearing, our reconnaissance squad arranged our tents in a rough circle. The detritus of the logged-out area included hundreds of well-seasoned stumps scattered amongst the tall, second-growth pines.

Non-tactical bivouac showing mountain tents, Camp Hale, Colorado

(Author photo)

They could easily be kicked over to provide fuel for social-hour campfires.

My mother was a gourmet baker and wasted no opportunity to use her ration stamps for sugar, flour, and butter to bake cookies and cakes. My father mailed packages on a weekly basis. He devised a system of protection for these goodies by inserting them in a padding of loose popcorn. Whole salamis, cans of sardines, jars of jelly, and boxes of crackers filled out whatever spaces remained. We feasted every night and bullshitted stories of our mostly imaginary sexual conquests. Exhaustion notwithstanding, we harmonized dirty lyrics to "My Blue Heaven" and other nostalgic favorites of the day. I had a passable baritone for a two-pack-a-day smoker. Johnny, with an excellent ear for harmony, added a sweet Irish tenor. The voices of the rest of the squad added or detracted, but everyone sang anyway.

We spent eight hours a day on skis, repeatedly lining up at the T-bar after the one-mile run down Cooper Hill, and swooped down the mountain again and again. Week after week we made the seven-mile Monday morning uphill march from camp to Cooper Hill, atop Tennessee Pass, then marched back to camp on Friday. On weekends, which began on Friday after retreat, when we had no pass to leave the post, trucks brought us up for recreational skiing. We could parallel ski to our heart's content. By midwinter, I could ski with the best of them. Well, almost.

Johnny had an edge when ski training began. He had several years' head start on me, having skied in a cemetery near his New Jersey home every chance he could. I can still imagine him zigzagging around the headstones as he zoomed across the tombs. I don't know how many residents turned over in their graves.

After a few weeks on Cooper Hill, I began to beat him in the improvised downhill races. Part of it may have been his eyesight. The Army had provided him with glasses, since he was nearsighted, but the GI-issue snow goggles didn't fit over them. He had to wear the goggles or risk snow blindness in the searing, snow-reflected light. He settled for dependence on his quick reactions to avoid the blurred shapes into which the pine trees deteriorated. Johnny hated the glasses, which he wore only

My best Army buddy Johnny Dolan (left) and Harry Weinsaft clowning around during training. Note that Johnny is holding his hated spectacles in his gloved hand. He would be killed in Italy.

(Author photo)

when seeing was essential. Amongst the many pictures I have of him, only one shows him with the spectacles on. That was taken at an outpost in Italy, just before our first big battle.

The final test of our skiing prowess was over a ski qualification course, a torturously convoluted five-mile stretch, mostly uphill along Pine Creek, from B Slope nearly to Cooper Hill. To the designers, it was a masochistic triumph. It encompassed every cross-country skiing hazard the warped minds of our instructors could find: repeated crossings (on skis) of the brush-choked flowing creek up a near-cliff escarpment, a path through house-sized boulders, blasting through a thick growth of aspens, down a rock-strewn slope, up an ice-covered logging road, and finally, getting across logs felled to clog narrow paths. And all this against the clock! We had one hour to complete the course, carrying a full rucksack and a rifle. I did it in fifty-one minutes. To Johnny's good-natured consternation, I beat him by a good five minutes. Later, when we huddled in exhaustion before the fire at our campsite, he said, "They must have tilted the damn thing downhill when you did it."

# 6:
# A Love Affair Takes Shape

October 1943 marked six months since I entered service and protocol dictated that I was due for my first furlough. So was Johnny and a new member of our company named Harry Weinsaft. Son of a Jewish-Austrian merchant, Harry and his family had been driven from Austria by the threat of Nazism and immigrated to New York in 1937. Harry had skied as a youth. When war broke out, Harry volunteered for the 10th and arrived at Camp Hale at about the same time I did. Harry became a wireman in the communications section of our company and soon attached himself to Johnny and me. I think the main attraction was Johnny's status as a fellow metropolitan New Yorker and mine as a fellow Jew. We decided to take our furloughs at the same time. The plan was that we would all take the *Rocket* from Denver to Chicago, and they would stay overnight at the railroad station to catch a New York Central train east the next day.

When we arrived at the station in Chicago, my parents, who met the train, would have none of that and insisted that Johnny and Harry stay overnight in our apartment. My brother gave up his twin bed in our bedroom for Johnny and slept on the floor. Harry stretched out on the living room sofa. But not before my mother put on a virtual banquet for all of us. The next morning they boarded the Clark Street trolley and continued their trip home.

Lois came in from California a few days later. We had been faithful in our promises to write to each other every day, and I was now convinced that she really was my one and only route to eternal happiness. When Lois and I accompanied a young cousin to a beauty parlor to get her hair done, I was just overwhelmed with her presence and kneeled down in the lobby to pop the question. I wasn't too surprised when she smiled and answered, "Yes."

My dad had a jeweler friend who made us an irresistible offer on a minuscule diamond, which I ceremoniously placed on her third finger, left hand. My dad's banker accepted my note for $125 (Dad co-signed), to be paid off at ten dollars a month. I mailed Dad a money order every payday, and he took care of the bank note.

I was hooked, and so was Lois. She returned to California when I headed back to Camp Hale. On my next furlough, she and her mother both came to Chicago, took an apartment, got jobs, and stayed. Her mother eventually moved back to San Francisco but my parents, as enchanted with Lois as I, treated her as if she was a daughter and made room for her in their apartment. My brother gave up his claim to the bedroom and moved onto a cot in the living room. Lois was now officially part of the family.

# 7: Frozen Asses

Back at Camp Hale in early November 1943, our first test of winter mobility was an exercise to simulate a lightning attack through the high, desolate country in midwinter. To lighten our ninety-pound loads, we formed three-man teams rather than the two normally prescribed. Johnny and I were joined by a communications man, which meant that three men crammed into a tent meant for two. But it also meant that we divided the load of rations, cooking equipment, tent, and poles amongst three men instead of two and could move much faster with the lighter loads. Our third man, George Fosberg, was nicknamed "Fearless" for the Fearless Fosdick character in the *Dick Tracy* comic strip. Lanky, rawboned, and easy-going, he accepted the name that came from the wry humor of operations sergeant Bob Fels. The *Dick Tracy* comic strip was all the rage in those days, due in no small part to the weird names of its characters. Fels had also labeled Leo Lepore, our foul-mouthed mess sergeant, "Leo the Lip," but only behind his back.

The area selected for the exercise was along Fall Creek, just east of the 14,000-foot Mount of the Holy Cross. Holy Cross and its adjacent ridges formed the western horizon visible from most of the elevated areas of Camp Hale. The trail ran just below it, at about 11,000 feet. In bitter cold, the battalion simulated a sweep down the valley to "capture" Lake Constantine, a frozen-over, mile-long glacial puddle. In the absence of the "vanquished enemy troops," we were permitted to pitch our tents and cook with gasoline-fueled mountain stoves. No campfires were permitted. That was an unnecessary precaution since we were above the timberline, and no wood was available for fires anyway.

This was one of our early experiences with mountain rations: A high-calorie feast of canned roast beef, several dehydrated vegetables, soup, and dessert. It was a huge improvement over the sparse enjoyment of C-rations. Normally ten men would share a day's rations, but we had the luxury of dividing it among only the nine men making up our entire group.

The author (left) and George "Fearless" Fosberg pose by one night's snowfall in the mountains above Camp Hale, December 1943.

(Author photo)

A small team from the Mountain Training Group acted as referees for the exercise and gave us the opportunity to see winter survival techniques at their finest. One of the team chopped a hole through the ice of Lake Constantine using a trench knife and in a flash plunged his bare hand into the thirty-two-degree water and came out with a thrashing trout, which he cooked for breakfast. What really creamed us was his act of widening the hole and then plunging into the water for his morning bath. Not in the least tempted to follow his example, the nine of us shared a #10 can of bacon and the powdery equivalent of three dozen eggs, cooked on our hissing mountain stove. The bath could wait.

The battalion, having broken camp, then "attacked" Fall River Pass with complete success, no casualties, and only one mishap. Our squad, in its reckless enthusiasm to reconnoiter for the next "battle," went too far beyond the pass and had to be retrieved by a panting referee. He was furious for having to race three additional miles on skis to fetch us back. Johnny and I were exulted. We had proven our mettle as military skiers, scouts, and mountain men. We could survive the very worst nature could throw at us. We felt everything from now on would be a cinch.

We were wrong....

# 8: "Wild" Weekend

Weekend passes took a variety of forms. In most cases, because of Camp Hale's isolation, passes began Friday night after inspection and retreat and ended at reveille on Monday morning. That left time to get to Denver, a four-hour trip by bus or car, before the dead of night or an unforeseen blizzard made travel too hazardous. The weekend train between Salt Lake City and Denver took a leisurely twelve hours, and the connection back to camp was often erratic. Denver was the preferred destination. It offered a great USO club, an amusement park crawling with girls in the summer, and lots of reasonably priced hotels.

Getting *to* Denver for a weekend was a real problem, though. Few had access to a car, and those who did charged ten or twelve dollars for a round trip. That was pretty stiff for a private making thirty dollars a month. In the midst of winter, a blizzard could leave you stranded atop Loveland Pass, or in Denver, facing an AWOL charge if you were unable to return to camp before reveille on Monday morning. The one daily scheduled bus had a capacity of about forty—somewhat inadequate to handle the thousands of GIs trying to get on board. Hitchhiking was a real gamble because gas rationing severely limited civilian travel. Johnny and I tried it only one time and managed to get a mere twenty-five miles before a black, bitterly cold night overtook us. We were standing on an isolated road until after midnight for a long time before a sympathetic deputy sheriff ferried us back to camp.

Denver's Kenmark Hotel was a favorite for those on limited budgets. Those flush with money from home checked in at the swanky Brown Palace. At the Kenmark, two of us could rent a room for about three dollars and would get dibs on the bed. Four or five buddies would fork over one or two dollars each for the privilege of sleeping on the floor, in a chair, or in a pillow-filled bathtub.

The main competition for girls (just looking for friendship, of course) came from the flyboys—the Lowry Field Air Corps ground-crew personnel—who wore the "Fifty-Mission crush" on their garrison caps. The "crush" on the hat was the result of hundreds of hours wearing earphones while on numerous missions. The ground crew never flew a single mission, but the effect was meant to impress the girls. We beat them all to hell by wearing our mountain jackets and ski pants with white gaiters. This was topped off by ski caps festooned with chromed crossed ski pins about two inches long. We explained to the girls the pins meant we were "ski captains."

The MPs didn't know what to make of us, but generally they left us alone. The MPs had enough trouble handling drunks without getting in a stew with rock-hard mountaineers.

Leadville, eighteen miles south of Camp Hale and at over 10,000 feet above sea level, was the closest town of any size, but it was a real hole. Leadville had once been a fabulous, wide-open mining town in the late 1800s and the silver mines there produced millionaires and millions of dollars worth of ore. But it had fallen on hard times in recent decades, even though its streets looked like a Hollywood set for a Western movie. For several months Leadville was completely off limits because of hordes of street-roaming whores. Even when it was cleaned up and those "working girls" were herded into brothels, the only thing to do there, besides getting laid, was getting drunk. Those were not attractive options for those of us who were raised to "live clean lives." The Army-sponsored films depicting the sorry consequences of venereal disease were also an effective deterrent. As far as Leadville was concerned, I retained my virginity.

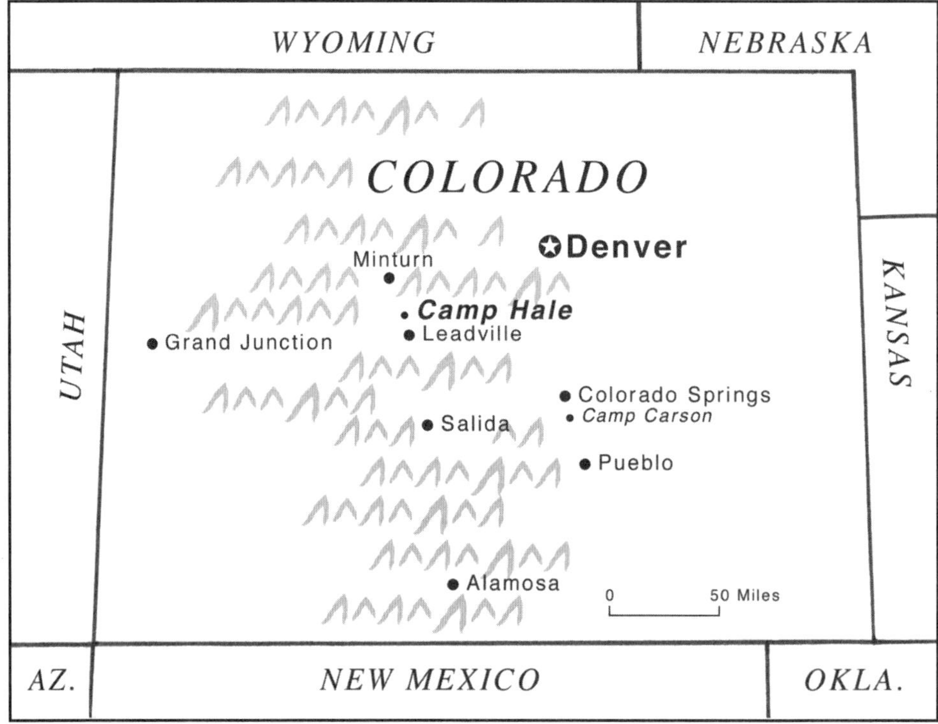


Colorado, showing location of Camp Hale, high in the Rockies

Salida, about 50 miles farther to the south, was the next alternative, and it was a reasonable train ride away. The attraction there was a cheap motel—five dollars for Johnny and me. Better yet, there was a huge public spring-fed hot pool. There, for about two bits (with GI discount), we could soak off a week's dirt and sweat in the summer, or send renewing warmth to our bones in the winter. There was also a dry-cleaning establishment that pressed uniforms while we waited, and a good barbershop with short lines of GIs waiting to get clipped for fifty cents. (GIs weren't expected to tip the barber.) The restaurants on the main street served huge breakfasts of juice, pancakes, eggs, bacon, toast, and coffee for less than two dollars. I think Johnny and I spent more weekends there than anyplace else. Life was wonderful.

One of our compatriots, Ted Rockafellow, grew up in Alamosa, just down the road from Salida, and he had a car. Johnny and I received a rare invitation to spend a weekend at his house, where his widowed mother treated us to some genuine home cooking. We chipped in for gas and took off for Alamosa on a Friday night. We stopped for a couple bottles of booze in Leadville and by the time we reached Salida, we were roaring drunk. Somehow, Ted avoided crashing into the cliffs bordering one side of the road or falling into the river rapids flowing on the opposite side. We were greeted and put to bed that night by a tongue-clucking Mrs. Rockafellow.

Just outside of Alamosa, surrounded by sand dunes, was a lake filled with hot springs. We spent most of Saturday soaking the booze out of our pores and making room for more imbibing that night. Alamosa boasted a junior college, and Ted guaranteed that it was populated only by horny and soldier-crazy females. He arranged to test that hypothesis by calling a girlfriend, who lined up dates for Johnny and me. We picked them up at suppertime, and embarked down the main street to one of Alamosa's coterie of eating establishments. My girl was nice enough. Being considerate of my pocketbook, she ordered only a hamburger and a shake. After supper, we piled back into Ted's car and headed out to the desert boondocks along a rutted, dusty trail. The seating was Ted and his girl in front, Johnny and I with our dates squeezed in back—mine on my lap. Ted found a parking spot on a small knoll where we could admire the moon. Although not completely comfortable, this was close enough to induce some first-class necking. The girls had unbending rules about where hand placement was acceptable, so nobody really "made out."

As the scene grew warmer, one of the girls mentioned the word "curfew." They explained they had to be in on time or face campus restrictions for a month. I suspected that we had been subjected to a well-rehearsed excuse, but horny or not, we were gentlemen. We dropped the girls off at their dorms in time to avoid a penalty, consoled ourselves with a few more swigs of booze, and headed back to Ted's house, our virginity intact. So much for a big Saturday night in Alamosa.

# 9:
# D Series

In late March 1944, the 10th Light Division virtually abandoned Camp Hale and spent the next month in the field. This was during Colorado's coldest winter in memory. In the season of deepest snow, we were forbidden to enter a building, build a fire, shower, or change clothes beyond what we carried on our backs. This became the now-infamous D-Series maneuvers.

On March 26th, Johnny and I rolled out of our sacks at 4 a.m., still groggy from a three-day weekend in Denver. Our skis were waxed, "red" as a base with "blue" to give additional traction for the long, uphill ski-march south to Mitchell Creek, just below Tennessee Pass, where the maneuvers would begin. It took over an hour to cram the rucksacks full with the gear necessary to sustain us. The list below comes from the 10th's history chart, reconstructed I'm sure from someone's faulty recollection. Two men shared some items, but it is generally agreed the field pack weighed ninety pounds.

Mountain tent, poles, aluminum stakes, and ropes
Double-down sleeping bags with wool liner, cotton inner liner, and poplin shell
Inflatable pad for under the hips
Extra socks (short cotton to hug the skin, light wool for moderate warmth, and bulky over-the-knee wool, all to be worn simultaneously)
Rubberized shoe-pacs for wet-snow camping
Extra felt shoe inner soles
Light cotton underwear to be worn on the skin, and wool long-johns to go over those
Rayon pile jacket (a poor man's fur coat)
Wool sweater and muffler
Poplin mountain jacket (which had multiple pockets, a hood which rolled up in the collar and a built-in pack in the back)
White gauntlets (to cover our gloves)

White coveralls (to pull over ski pants)
White rucksack cover for use in "combat" situations
Toilet kit (razor, shaving cream, toothbrush and paste, comb, and manicure tools)
Mess kit
Mountain stove, fuel, and cook-set
Ski wax
Ski climbers–climbing "skins"
Flashlight and candles
Matches and cigarettes
Miniature whisk broom (characteristically called a mountain brush)
Rifle cleaning kit
Chamois cold-weather facemask
And whatever else we could cram in.

My rucksack's outside pockets bulged with candy bars, chewing gum, a salami from home…and a couple of oranges the mess sergeant had managed to "steal" for me in exchange for a few slices of salami. Just under the top canvas flap, a pair of fifteen-inch-long miniature snowshoes formed a pair of wings to give me deep-snow flotation if I broke a ski.

Hanging from grommet-reinforced holes on my rucksack were my bayonet, entrenching tool, and canteen. My rifle's rear sling swivel clipped onto a hook, its barrel strapped in place by a half-inch-wide woven belt so it nestled snugly along the rucksack frame. The muzzle and bore were kept dry with a snap-on canvas cover, through which a bullet could be fired.

The web pistol belt around my waist suspended a first-aid kit, my compass case, and a non-GI foot-long trench knife that my uncle had fashioned from a case-hardened metal file. I used it throughout the war as a can opener, and it stayed sharp despite the abuse.

I wore the customary three pairs of socks inside my mountain boots. Other clothing included cotton jockey-style underwear and wool long-johns, and wool ski pants under cotton poplin mountain pants. The upper torso was shielded by a cotton undershirt, wool undershirt, wool shirt, and reversible (to white) hooded parka. My hands were layered with fingerless wool wristlets, wool mittens with a "trigger finger," and finally, leather-palmed poplin gauntlets that fastened above the wrist. I wore my ski cap's earflaps down, with the sun goggles fastened around the band. The rest of the clothing, to be donned when we stopped moving for any length of time and cooled down, was in the rucksack. Hanging on one shoulder were my binoculars. A musette bag with my S-2 paraphernalia crossed over the other. It carried maps of the area, a message pad, pencils, and a protractor to help plot "enemy" positions.

The author all packed up with no place to go.
(This is what 90 pounds of rucksack looks like.)

(Author photo)

Today's supply of the heatable C-rations bulged out of the inner pockets of my parka, stuffed there to keep from freezing. My normal weight of 140 pounds was now 230. Standing up really meant hunching awkwardly forward to keep from falling over backward. Our steel helmets ended up perched on top of the rucksacks—skiing was hard enough under that load without a metal tub on our heads.

When we paused for a ten-minute rest once every hour, we were supposed to divest ourselves of that load, but trying to get it all remounted was just too difficult. The compromise was to find a nearby embankment on which we could lean with the weight of the rucksack suspended by the earth. As an alternative, we learned that two men could take turns pulling one another erect before resuming the march.

We crossed the line of departure (Camp Hale's south gate) at 8 a.m., took a few steps, and came to a screeching halt. Some genius operations officer had given the whole division, over 14,000 men, a simultaneous marching time, and a Los Angeles-sized traffic jam froze us in place. The early morning temperature hovered close to thirty-nine degrees BELOW zero, and a new snowfall began, turning us into dusty statues. Pairs of energetic MPs finally got the traffic sorted out, and the long columns began their slow, uphill shuffle toward a month-long icy hell.

The approach march to the maneuver area was under non-tactical conditions, with HQ Company leading the battalion, followed by the line companies and weapons company. As battalion scouts, Johnny and I took a hundred-yard lead over the rest of the column to fend off and caution what few civilian cars might come along Highway 24, our initial marching route. The remainder of the S-2 squad fell in with the rest of HQ Company.

The seven-man S-2 squad was a heterogeneous group of enlisted men volunteers lead by a wiry, taciturn 1st Lieutenant John "Jessie" James. He was the battalion S-2 (combat intelligence) officer and company commander as well. The men in our squad were scout observers, which is a pretty descriptive name for what we did.

Our training concentrated on methods of getting close to the enemy, undetected, to see what he was doing, then reporting observed FACTS back to HQ. Speculation was prohibited unless clearly labeled by "I guess." The facts were then passed back to higher elements, where they were evaluated. Conclusions of enemy "intentions and capabilities" were deduced or—more accurately—guessed at.

Several methods of gathering information were used. Observation posts (OPs) and listening posts (LPs) were manned, well hidden or disguised, most often beyond our own lines. (Later in Italy, we were ocassionally accompanied or replaced by German-speaking men who could translate overheard conversations of enemy soldiers. We learned to differentiate between the sounds of motor vehicles so we could identify if it was an unseen tank, a truck, or a motorcycle. Patrols were often necessary to ferret out German positions, minefields, or take prisoners for interrogation.) The safest time for patrols was at night, although the darkness made any movement toward a specific target area much more difficult. As scouts, we were expected to be expert in every technique of information gathering.

Our squad consisted of Tibor Mikes, the S-2 sergeant, and six PFCs. (We never counted Jessie as part of the squad because of his dual designation of company commander.)

Tibor's Hungarian accent was crisp and pronounced, but his command of languages also included some French, German, and Russian. They clearly announced his huge intelligence. Short, wiry, and extremely athletic, he had been a high-ranking tennis amateur in his native land. He constantly reminded us of that by bragging of his extremely well-developed right pectoral muscle, a result, he insisted, of years of playing right-handed tennis. By nature he was a perfectionist, and insisted that HIS squad would be the best S-2 group in the division, and we would practice and practice our skills until we became the best. Under his leadership, that came true. In test after test, our squad scored at or near the top. He was as relentless as a sergeant could be, but he was never unfair and could be depended upon as a friend.

Besides Johnny and me, there were four other PFCs:

Thirty-something Joe Carr was easy-going, stocky, square-jawed, and a former Baltimore milkman. He was the old man of our squad. Ten years or so of lugging cases of milk up apartment steps gave him a terrific pair of legs. Only rarely did his years betray his ability to keep up. He was given to muttering, "Fuckinsonofabitch" under his breath. This was usually enough to defuse any stressful circumstance.

Bob L, who had a Harvard accent, appeared to be somewhat effeminate. He was, in our estimation, a complete oddball, and we unfairly tormented him with practical jokes. He called us "Bahstads," and constantly threatened to have "mothaw" pull a few strings to get him transferred to a more cultured group. In fairness, he was as good a soldier and scout as any of us, but boys will be boys.

Wally Barron, a laconic ex-Maine forest ranger, was tall, lean as a coyote, and had a dry sense of humor. He could move through the woods, without crinkling a leaf, to pet a wild deer. He was nearly as old as Joe Carr the milkman, but we never regarded Wally as an old man. Our constant awe of his outdoorsmanship probably contributed to that.

Bert Hirtle, blond and handsome, was a loner who would wander off in the woods for a weekend and come back refreshed. We speculated that if you turned him loose in the wilderness with just a knife and a piece of string, he could trap a rabbit with a snare, build a fire "boy scout" style, construct an igloo in the winter or a hammock in a lean-to in the summer. He could live totally off the land.

Later, Hirtle went to the regimental S-2 squad, probably because he was our best scout. Bob L, to our great relief, had his mother pull some strings and went to a higher HQ as somebody's aide. Wally, also a top scout, earned two more stripes and moved to our weapons company when a change in our TO (Table of Organization) opened a slot for him to become the Machine Gun Sergeant.

We lost three well-trained men over an extended time, later replaced with some difficulty. The first replacement was Sherman Platt, scion of a well-known publishing family. We soon lost him to OCS (Officer Candidate School), where he went in response to family pressure to become something more than a mere enlisted GI.

Edwin Nedoszytko followed. A pleasant, baby-faced character from New York, he had only average ability as a skier, but he was bright and personable and immediately became the mascot of our squad. We fell all over ourselves to bring him up to date on our S-2 skills, and he succeeded in integrating himself rather quickly. We never called him anything but "Ned."

The other new man was Curley L, so named because he was nearly bald. Curley had entered the Army as a volunteer to escape the wrath of the IRS, which had mercilessly pursued him for allegedly taking liberties with his deductions as a traveling salesman. Under the rules then in force, the IRS could not hassle anyone in the armed forces. Curly was bright and aggressive. He soon became thoroughly integrated into the squad.

Our original bunch—Joe Carr, Bob L., Wally Barron, Bert Hirtle, Johnny, and me—all slogged up the hill together and began D-Series. For the first couple of days, we were full of piss and vinegar. We bitched enough to be recognizable as GIs, but "elan" carried the day. Even the crushing thirty-degrees-below-zero weather could not dent our spirits. We were jubilantly, supremely confident of our ability to overcome whatever Mother Nature could throw at us.

The Army was a different matter.

The first "attack" was aimed at Homestake Peak, at 13,211 feet, one of the high points within the camp boundary. Increasingly aware of the ninety-pound burdens, we headed south toward the junction with Bennett Gulch and turned east into the wilderness. Slowed by weapons platoons dragging their intolerable loads on toboggans, or wading through deep drifts on snowshoes, or stopped by the tracked weasels, which slithered from side to side on the narrow mule trail, we stopped for the night near the opening into Wurt's Ditch. The ditch is a man-made canal about the width of a jeep and four or five feet deep. It meanders for about five miles at the 10,000-foot contour level, and may originally have been a water-carrying project for a now-defunct mine. For our purposes, it served well as a defiladed approach to our objective. It served the weasels as a road, fortuitously lacking the snow-drift-hidden tree stumps that threw the weasel's treads, leaving the vehicles sputtering helplessly in the ruts.

We bedded down comfortably after cutting a foot-thick insulating layer of pine boughs to serve as mattresses under our mountain tents. Since we were in the approach march, our field kitchens were operational, and we had the luxury of a hot meal. The cooks set up big garbage cans of chemically treated water heated by

Here I am, heating up a canteen-cup full of pre-Starbucks coffee over a fire in the high country of Colorado. The water boiled quickly at this altitude but cooled off even faster.

(Author photo)

immersible, gasoline-fueled, inefficient heaters that barely kept the water hot. The procedure was to dip aluminum mess kits in the water and raise their temperature above the ambient thirty-degrees-below-zero to a point where the food wouldn't immediately freeze to the metal. The food, heated in huge pots balanced precariously on gasoline-powered stoves, was sloshed onto the mess kits, and we then had three or four minutes to find a fallen tree, straddle it as a dining table, and wolf down the meal before it turned to icy mush.

Too often breakfast consisted of infamous SOS (shit on a shingle); i.e., watery chipped beef slopped on a slab of barely toasted bread, and bitter coffee. Dinner was often a stew, with adequate amounts of meat and potatoes supplemented with a vegetable.

Our daily food allotment, which included a C- or K-ration lunch, was said to contain over 3,000 calories and provided us with enough energy to survive the cold and effort required of mountain warfare. We made a second trip to the mess line for coffee, preheated the cup by dipping it in "hot" water, ladled in the instant coffee, and relished the warmth radiating onto our bare hands as we gulped the rapidly cooling liquid. Afterward, a little snow rubbed into the mess kits removed most of the crud. Another quick dip into each of the two water solutions left the kits ready for the next meal. Miraculously, with this loose regimen of health precautions, virtually no one became sick from food poisoning. Or maybe it was just too damn cold for bacteria to survive.

Getting into the sack was another ritual that only experience could teach. Typically, I gave the mountain tent a final check. The ropes went to aluminum stakes that were buried in the snow or were tied to nearby trees using only half hitches—NEVER knots that would freeze into a rigid mass. The ropes had to have just the right amount of slack. Too much, and even the weight of a light snowfall would collapse the tent. Too little slack, and the stakes would pull loose with the same result. Tubular vents extended from each end of the tent and were intended to insure fresh air circulation.

I thrust my skis vertically into the snow at the tent entrance or leaned them against a bipod formed by poles. Even a light snowfall would quickly conceal a pair of skis carelessly left on the ground. My mountain brush flicked the accumulated snow from clothing, boots, and rucksack before I crawled through the tunnel entrance.

Sitting in the dark, I inflated my hip pad by mouth, removed the sleeping bag (AKA "fart sack") from the rucksack, unrolled it, and unzipped it as I stretched its full length along the tent floor. Sitting on the opened bag, I undid the straps on my ski gaiters and unlaced my boots, which were shoved into the very bottom of the sleeping bag. Then came layer after layer of clothing, some of which I rolled up to remain in the bag with me as a pillow. The rest became "ground cloths," but inside the bag, as further shields from the snow-covered frozen tundra.

Next, I stuffed the partially emptied rucksack at the foot end of the tent, to be used as a mattress for my feet. Often, by the flickering light of our hoarded candle shielded in an empty C-ration can, I would get off a short note to Lois before exhaustion overcame me and my eyelids began to droop. Stripped down to only one pair of socks and my long-johns, I zipped the sleeping bag closed and settled down for a few hours' sleep. My tent-mate, inevitably Johnny, was suffering the same series of convoluting contortions in the other half of our tiny tent, but with his head at my feet.

Sometimes, GODDAMMIT, I forgot to go take a leak before going through this elaborate process. A big decision awaited me then. Should I hold it until I couldn't any longer (at 3 a.m.), chance waiting until morning, or just put on my pants, boots, and parka again to make a dash for a place to turn the snow yellow, or what? Too often, I had to make that agonizing decision.

Getting up in the morning was even worse. It was the coldest part of the day, and if I got through the night without pissing, the need was now urgent. If my socks from yesterday were dry as a result of the overnight session in my sleeping bag, they were put in my rucksack and fresh ones donned. If they were still damp, they would end up around my waist between my underwear and shirt for an all-day drying session with body heat. The other clothes I unrolled from their pillow or retrieved from their ground-cloth positions and put them on before I opened the sleeping bag. It was usually about thirty degrees below zero. Last, with the sleeping bag now unzipped, out came the ski boots. Then a mad dash for the latrine.

That could be an experience in itself. The expression was, "How do you get two inches through six inches of clothing?" Those who couldn't sported a mantle of yellow ice around the ski pants fly all day. Bowel movements were as challenging. Digging a GI-style latrine in solid icy ground was impossible in winter, so "watch your step" areas became the accepted norm. Squatting while holding on to a small tree in front of you required exquisite balancing techniques. A few shovelfuls of snow quickly returned the area to its pristine beauty. I don't know if all the bacteria survived the cold, but I never heard of sewage-spread disease while I was at Camp Hale. This was the origin of the skier's commandment, "Don't eat the yellow snow."

If the tactical situation permitted, the cooks would have started breakfast at some ungodly hour and had it ready when we staggered from our tents. If we were under "combat" conditions, but out of sight of the "enemy," we warmed our C- or K-rations as best we could on the little mountain stoves. That was done by filling a pot repeatedly with snow to be melted and finally boiled. The can of ham and eggs would be placed in the boiling water until it was thawed enough to eat. In daylight hours, if we had used up our small supply of mountain-stove fuel, we could use the waxed cardboard K-ration box as fuel for a small, smokeless fire. It gave off just enough heat to boil a canteen cupful of water, into which we put the can to be warmed. Presto, we had hot water to mix with the powdered coffee as well.

Finally, we buried the garbage in the snow and struck camp. That meant deflating the hip pad, stuffing it and the sleeping bag into a somehow shrunken rucksack, and then folding the tent. The frozen accumulation of breathing moisture in the tent at night left the nylon fabric with the flexibility of tank armor. Somehow, Johnny and I, with great common effort, would get it rolled into a vague shape and stuffed under the flap of one of our rucksacks. The stakes, poles, and ropes went into the other. With luck, the whole process of beginning a day could be accomplished in one tortuous hour.

The battalion was then poised to attack Homestake Peak from the east along the Continental Divide. The supporting HQ troops poured down Wurt's Ditch to the north. Some of us hitched a ride by being pulled by ropes trailing from the weasels. For those closest to the vehicle, the engine's hot exhaust gave welcome relief from the cold, but the overpowering carbon monoxide fumes quickly killed off that sport.

After a week or so of feints and attacks on the peak and adjacent areas, we were deemed to have been victorious and re-assembled at the frozen marsh near Mitchell Creek. I made a terrible blunder that night. I left my sweat-soaked boots outside my sleeping bag and awoke to find them solidly frozen. No amount of pounding,

An M-29 cargo carrier known as the "weasel."

(U.S. Army photo)

The author on mountain maneuvers at Camp Hale, Colorado, 1944

(Author photo)

twisting, or kneading restored their pliability. I spent the next several hours skiing precariously with unlaced frozen boots. I deserved frozen toes or a broken ankle but survived with just a bit more wisdom.

The next phase of D-Series was an attack on Ptarmigan Hill, a treeless 12,154-foot peak standing at the head of Resolution Creek, six miles northeast of camp.

The assembly area for the attack lay behind a nameless 11,800-foot mountain nestled in the valley of Pearl Creek, which branched eastward from Resolution Creek. We marched there directly from Mitchell Creek, passing through Camp Hale without pause. The battalion set up a tactical situation camp in the deep snow—no fires, no lights, cold rations, and no tents. That is, except for the command post.

Before Johnny and I could dig our way into a snow bank and form a cave floored with pine boughs, Tibor and Lieutenant James called us into the CP tent to give us a scouting mission. By rapidly dimming light, Jessie pointed to our position on my 1-to-25,000-scale map, to the "enemy" positions to the north, and to the intervening ridge.

"We're sitting here like a duck on a pond," Jessie said. "I want you and Dolan to go to the top of this ridge to our north and see what's going on. We have nobody between us and the 'enemy' occupying Ptarmigan Peak, and I don't want any surprises. Set up an OP and listening post, but stay out of sight. There'll be a pretty good moon tonight. If you see or hear anything, try to get a handle on it, and skedaddle back here. We're under radio silence and I don't have enough wire to give you a field telephone. Get going, NOW!"

We were assigned to climb in the dark, on skis, through unexplored terrain, the almost 2,000 feet to the top of the unnamed mountain between us and Ptarmigan Peak, and get set up without being detected. To make sure we stayed awake and didn't get too comfortable, we were to drop our packs here, taking only enough clothing to keep us from freezing.

Just after sundown, Johnny and I slipped climbers onto our skis and began the long, arduous traverse towards the top. The powder snow was very deep. We had run some training missions along this ridge during the summer, under the thirty-foot-high pines, only six feet of which now protruded above the drifts. The going became so difficult that we took turns breaking trail, changing the lead every few hundred feet. We paused frequently, breathing hard, straining to listen for clues of human presence. Even our own troops in the coulee below seemed utterly silent. Our battalion slept as if in the Valley of the Dead. It was relatively warm, probably just above zero, so we were able to strip down to just our mountain jackets and stuffed our pile jackets and sweaters into the narrow pack built into the back of the jacket.

We reached the ridge top in a couple of hours and for concealment silently stomped a waist-deep depression in the snow in the shadow of a tree just inside the timberline. As we cooled down from the exertion of the climb, we donned our sweaters but kept our jackets handy if needed. We laid our skis across a snow bench inside the trench, which gave us effective insulation, and settled in.

No sound or lights emanated from "enemy" territory. We repeatedly scoped across the valley, peering into the moonlit vales for ski tracks, snow caves, or some sign of activity. At intervals I cheated and lit up a cigarette while huddling in the bottom of the trench. The flare of the Zippo and glow of the cigarette were effectively concealed by the spare jacket. Neither of us uttered a word. We spent the next few hours in silent contemplation of the exquisite beauty surrounding us. The pristine whiteness magnified the moonlight, so every undulation of the terrain took on exaggerated character. The shadows became three-dimensional Rorschach blots. Except for the wind's faint whisper through the trees below and the rustle of our own clothing, our breathing was the only discernable sound. The imaginary enemy, camped behind Ptarmigan two miles to our north, did not stir. No enemy patrols or raids, real or imaginary, disturbed our solitude.

At the first streak of dawn, with climbers already stripped from our skis for a fast getaway, we headed downhill toward friendly lines. The breathtaking, two-mile zigzag run through untracked deep powder was reward enough for the sleepless night. It was that kind of enchantment that kept most of us in the 10th. The magical synthesis of beauty, adventure, and the exultation of the physical conquest of nature without destroying it was at work.

Buried not too deeply in our psyche, there also lurked a boyish hint of machismo and mischief. We paused momentarily on a knoll overlooking the bivouac, unchallenged by any lookouts. We watched as the company went about its wake-up business, unmindful of any outside interference.

Johnny looked at me and I at him. Smirks spread across our faces. "Let's gettum," he said, and with banshee howls and a guttural imitation of machine-gun fire, we swooped down on the startled troops.

"Gotcha all," we howled, and skidded to a halt at the CP to report, "No sign of enemy activity." Not one officer thought it was funny.

We rejoined the S-2 squad as they bit into their cold K-ration breakfast of chopped ham and eggs. The officers were too close to us for the squad to join in a guffaw, but a few carefully timed winks assured us of their support. Somebody noted that it was Easter Sunday. A barrage of quarter-sized snowflakes began to fall.

# 10: Easter Sunday

We spent the day in a fitful stop-and-go, uphill ski march toward Ptarmigan Pass, the crest of which was held by the "enemy." The huge snowflakes settled on us, melting into huge, growing splotches of water that penetrated even our tightly woven parkas. The midday temperatures rose above the freezing point. By late afternoon, rivulets of melted snow were running through all the layers of our gear and mixing with perspiration. Our parkas, pile jackets, sweaters, shirts, and longjohns had been switched from rucksacks to bodies at every pause in the climb. Each item was now soaking wet.

As the evening sun dipped below the adjacent ridges, the temperature dropped toward zero, and a mantle of ice began to crystallize on our shoulders. Darkness caught us just above timberline. The word came to "dig in" and settle down for the night under tactical conditions. That meant no tents and no fires.

I slipped out of my rucksack and used my skis to pound out a rectangular trench about seven feet long, three feet wide, and two feet deep in the wispy powder snow. I made a dozen or more trips to a sparse grove of pines a hundred yards below to break off an armful of boughs with which to line my bed. With a foot-high mattress of boughs to lift me off the bottom, I rolled out my sleeping bag and—wet clothes and all—squirmed inside.

Laboriously I twisted and turned as I pulled the parka over my head and laid it on the base of the sleeping bag so my body heat would help dry it. My pile jacket, sweater, and shirt followed, as did my poplin mountain pants and wool ski pants. All of them were sopping wet. Survival tomorrow depended upon getting some of the moisture evaporated by body heat. I reached out of the bag for my rucksack, pulled a frozen K-ration into the sleeping bag, opened it, and managed to down a frozen supper of chopped ham, crackers, and a candy bar. As I reached outside to throw the can away, Tibor hovered over me with an unwelcome message.

"Daneman, our squad has CP security tonight, one hour each man. You take the first shift. Dolan will relieve you."

Cursing silently, I re-donned the wet clothes and struggled through the hip-deep snow to Johnny's trench dug a few yards away, carrying one end of an extra tent rope. "Tie this to your peter," I said. "I'll yank it when it's your turn." He tied it instead to one hand.

For the next hour I sat perched on my rucksack, shivering in my snow-foxhole while watching for "enemy" patrols that I knew would never come, at least not that night. When the glowing hands of my watch showed that I had suffered through my assigned hour, I yanked on the cord connecting me to Johnny. He moaned and groaned as I yanked repeatedly until he awakened for his shift. Finally, I crawled into my bag and stripped for a few hours' rest.

Morning found me buried under another foot of snow through which Tibor prodded his ski pole to wake me up. He knew where my head was by the position of my implanted skis. The twenty-minute dressing job into icy, still-damp clothes done, I gulped a K-ration of chopped ham and eggs and went through the torture of trying to put an ice-crusted, ten-cubic-foot sleeping bag into a six-cubic-foot rucksack. I struggled into the rucksack by positioning it a few feet uphill of my body and getting Johnny to hoist me vertical. I reciprocated, and we joined the line of troopers beginning the final ascent of Ptarmigan Hill.

The narrowness of the ridge restricted the multiple cutbacks needed to make the climb on the fresh, deep powder, so the command was given to put the climbing skins over our skis. That was another experimental torture. Fortunately, I had moved the skins to an outer rucksack pocket, but they had received a major soaking in yesterday's wet snow and were frozen solid. With great difficulty, I pried them out of their curl and got them mounted on the ski bottoms—backwards, with the strands of rabbit hair pointing uphill. Exasperated, I re-did them correctly and joined the line of white-clad men moving directly up the ridge, albeit at a snail's pace.

For a few hours, we maneuvered over the bare ridge, simulating recons here and there, manning observation and listening posts. At noon, we took shelter from a howling wind in a stand of timber just below the tree line. I was determined to eat my first unfrozen meal in days and prepared my "kitchen" for the event. In what looked like the shallowest part of a snow bank, I trampled the snow as firmly as possible, broke off a few boughs, and laid a base for cooking. I tore the waxed K-rations box into pieces, which I pyramided about two inches high on the boughs, and lit them with my Zippo. As the fire progressed, I stuffed my canteen cup full of snow, which I refilled several times as the snow melted. In a relatively few minutes I had a simmering cup of water. I dropped a can of chopped ham into the water, which at this altitude boiled at about 180 degrees. As the last fragment of the waxed carton turned to ash, I had generated both a hot lunch and enough boiling water for a cup of instant coffee. Soaking the concrete-hard chocolate bar before adding the Nescafe softened it enough to eat without the threat of broken teeth.

A nameless GI attempted to follow my example but built his fire under the sweeping snow-covered branches of a tree. As he melted the water, the heat rose and dislodged a huge clump of snow from a limb, dousing both him and the fire. Another lesson in cold-weather survival well learned.

Orders for the next phase of D-Series filtered down to the battalion. Now we were to ski-march to the bottom of Resolution Creek and reassemble there for an attack on Gold Park several miles to the north of Camp Hale.

We reached the assembly area, just outside the camp, in late afternoon and found that two men of our company who had spent most of the D-Series home on furlough had returned just in time to await our arrival at the terminus of the creek. They had used the day to construct a log-and-pine-bough lean-to just large enough to house our entire squad. That night we slept under the luxury of a real roof, albeit porous enough to read by the moonlight, and I scratched out a brief letter to Lois. It read, in part, "*My darling — The last 24 hours have been the toughest I've ever spent. I've never been so completely exhausted — never hurt in so many places — never needed sleep more – – never needed your soft shoulder more....*"

Exhausted S-2 squad members during the grueling D-Series maneuvers at Camp Hale, Colorado, March 1944. Shown left to right: Tibor Mikes, me, Johnny Dolan, Wally Barron, and Joe Carr.

(Author photo)

We were further blessed by a short delay in the attack, which gave us a chance to drape our clothing on tree limbs to dry in the now-abundant sunshine.

The rising temperatures of the nascent spring brought with them a mixed blessing. Diminishing morning darkness brought us awake in almost balmy surroundings. Our teeth no longer chattered uncontrollably as we struggled out of our sleeping bags. We were still in a tactical situation, though, so the company kitchen was inoperative, and we remained on K-rations. Morning coffee remained reasonably lukewarm. But the warmer temperatures also brought us rapidly melting snow and the consequential mud.

Johnny discovered the penalty for choosing to wear his glasses instead of his ski goggles for a few days. His eyes became inflamed from the sun reflecting off the snow, and at sick call he was diagnosed with snow blindness and transported to the station hospital. I managed to wangle permission to visit him there and was subjected to glances of horror by the nurses in pristine white garb. I stole a peek at myself in a mirror and recoiled in shock. I hadn't shaved or washed in weeks, and my face was peeling from the constant exposure to the sun and wind.

A kindly nurse led me to a washroom, provided me with soap and a washcloth, and I made the attempt to look civilized. The dead skin peeled off in layers and, although bearded, left me with the pinkish hue of a newborn baby. It also hurt like hell, so the nurse provided me with some kind of soothing lotion. Then, back to the lean-to. Johnny rejoined us the next day, no worse for the experience.

The hiatus in maneuvers ended soon enough. The now snowless trails meant we had to shoulder ninety-pound packs with the skis fastened on the rucksacks in the form of an "A." Picture the tips joined by a strap, poised overhead with the skis' tails behind our heels, only a few inches above the ground. Thus festooned, we set off toward Gold Peak at the headwaters of Homestake Creek to complete D-Series.

The final week was a cinch except for the agony of the weighted packs whose straps cut deep crevices into our shoulders with the hip-frame pressed inexorably into our backs and the burning torment of enormous blisters from walking mile after mile in boots intended only for skiing and rock climbing. We went through the motions of night patrolling, did a few quick marches to elude an imaginary foe, and swooped down on unsuspecting enemy positions. By now it was all automatic. We had it down pat. We were damn good soldiers and we knew it. The D-Series had proved it. At last we headed down the slick muddy trails back to Camp Hale.

My feet were now so blistered that the pain of walking under the ninety-pound burden was excruciating. As a matter of pride, I refused a seat in Lieutenant James' jeep, offered when he saw how I was struggling to make it home. In a demonstration of the egalitarian attitude that permeated our company, half a dozen men stripped me of my pack, skis, and rifle, and took turns lugging the load for the final mile. At least I made it back on my own two feet…barely.

In the barrack at last, I managed to dump my gear on my almost forgotten bunk bed and hobbled to the battalion aid station to get some attention for my nearly destroyed feet. I wasn't the only one. I waited in line while several dozen others had their blisters attended to. Mine were unbelievable. After removing my boots, the medics discovered that a bloody residue had glued my socks to my feet. Immersion in a bucket of warm water dissolved that mess. The medics were then able to carefully peel the socks from my feet and apply an antibiotic salve and a layer of gauze bandages. I was offered three days of "light duty" but I politely refused, knowing that meant three days of KP. It was Friday, and the two-day weekend would be enough to restore my feet. Besides, I was a rugged ski trooper, wasn't I?

A great shot of all the officers and enlisted men in our company.
How young we all were then! (I am in the middle row, 7th from the right.)

Dolan
Platt
Weinsaft
Me
t. James
LePore

## 11: Deep in the Heart of...

The rest of the spring in 1944, while a million Allied troops in England were preparing to invade Hitler's Fortress Europe, was spent almost leisurely in Camp Hale by the 10th. In April, I had another furlough with Johnny and Harry accompanying me as far as Chicago. Once more they camped out at my home overnight before catching the train to New York. Lois was now a permanent resident of Chicago. As her mother prepared to move back to San Francisco, Lois had made it clear that she wanted to stay in Chicago to be near me when I came in on furlough. My mom and dad insisted that she move in with them, giving her my old bedroom. This cozy arrangement meant that Lois was always home for me whenever I had a furlough.

My brother Jerry didn't wait until his eighteenth birthday and enlisted in the Navy. With unbelievable luck, he took boot camp training at the Great Lakes Naval Training Station just north of Chicago and trained as a radar technician at Navy Pier, near downtown Chicago. That meant he was home every weekend. Lois then had to willingly relinquish her claim to the bedroom, ceding it to Jerry and making the living room sofa her bed.

Back at Camp Hale, the S-2 squad continued to hone its skills. We made frequent conditioning hikes and spent time learning the special skills the other men in headquarters had become expert in. I went to radio school and learned how to lay and splice communication wires, and then send messages by Morse code. At a school for the Ammunition and Pioneering Platoon, I became familiar with mine laying and clearing, and booby-trap construction and disarming. The anti-tank platoon was armed with a 75mm howitzer, a 37mm cannon, and a .50-caliber machine gun. I learned the assembly, aiming, and firing of each. By early May 1944, with D-Series and the fine-tuning behind us, we expected the call to combat at any time.

The battle in Italy had not gone well for almost a year. Ever since the Allies had leaped from Sicily to the mainland in September 1943, the Germans had put up a stubborn resistance—despite the fact that Mussolini had been ousted and the king of Italy declared his country neutral. In the fall of 1943, after slogging for months from one mountain to another, Mark Clark's U.S. Fifth Army had slammed up against Monte Cassino and the monastery there, 100 miles south of Rome. The fighting became a deadly stalemate. Even an "end run" up the coast to Anzio that was supposed to have ended the stalemate became bogged down. Finally, at the end of May 1944, just before D-Day in Normandy, the Allies managed to break free and Rome was captured on June 4. The Germans retreated north of Rome but didn't show any signs that they were about to give up, and we just KNEW we would be dispatched shortly to finish the job. The rumors were reinforced by orders to pack up everything and, by alerts, prepare for a move on short notice. Where were we going? If anyone knew, they weren't telling.

Early one June morning, we shouldered our bulging barracks bags and—like sheep—were hustled off to a waiting troop train at the Pando station whose destination was unknown to us.

Interminable hours later, perhaps it was a few days, the train screeched to a halt at a siding. We were warned to NOT use the train's toilet facilities until we were well underway again (the toilets flushed directly onto the tracks). It was barely past dawn, but we saw dozens of women laden with doughnuts and cups of steaming coffee waiting for us along the track. We were permitted to detrain and were inundated by the friendly faces and eager hands passing out the goodies. We learned we were in Wichita Falls, Texas, and this was the customary welcome of Texas ladies for soldiers passing through.

Later that day, we were disgorged into the searing heat of Camp Swift, east of Austin, Texas. Snatched from the cool beauty of the Rockies about to bloom into a magnificent summer, we were ingloriously dumped into the cauldrons of hell. We hated it. We also learned that on June 6th the Allies had invaded Normandy, France, but without the 10th Light Division.

To get us quickly acclimated to the heat, we were almost immediately ordered to complete a long, daytime march. With our superb conditioning, and sated with sea-level oxygen, we thought it would be a cinch. We were wrong. I thought I had been miraculously saved when I was ordered to take a shortcut less than five miles up McDade Road—to the point where the rest of the company would finish the halfway point of the hike. The only catch was that I would lead a mule, laden with five-gallon cans of water and the Lister bag, which I was to set on a tripod and dispense the water.

The mule had his own idea of how to proceed down the dusty road. He sat down, and only by dint of a kick in the belly and a firm grip of his halter was I able to make him budge. I spent the whole five miles literally dragging the mule and his load. I doubt that I averaged even one mile per hour.

The final destination was a sparse grove of trees just thick enough to provide

The main gate at Camp Swift, Texas. It didn't take us long to hate this place.

(U.S. Army photo)

some shade for the exhausted, footsore troops when they arrived at their halfway mark. Setting up the Lister bag was easy. First Sergeant Harry Leisentreit showed his true-blue colors when he drove up to the site in his jeep bearing a garbage can filled with ice. It didn't take long to have ice water awaiting the arrival of the company.

Within the first two hours of their departure from our barracks, most of our company was strung out, prostrate alongside the dusty road, suffering the first stages of heat exhaustion. As the men straggled in, weary and disconsolate, to collapse in heaps, I ran around gathering canteens and refilling them with ice water.

We assumed the Army had decided to kill us off and make it look like a training accident. In the following weeks, morale dropped precipitously, and the imposition of a new Table of Organization didn't help. A few thousand non-mountaineers, non-skiers, were added to our ranks to beef up new heavy-weapons companies and artillery battalions. In mountain warfare, they would be issued snowshoes for winter marches, so the lack of skiing skills was not of consequence. We strongly resented the new training techniques to survive hot weather and "flatlander" combat.

Our Texas civilian hosts graciously overlooked our northern hostility and welcomed us with open arms. The USO in Austin was always filled with beautiful University of Texas coeds, and folks in the surrounding towns welcomed us into their homes. Gradually, we came to appreciate the warmth of their reception.

Grudgingly, we added the new skills and conditioning to our arsenal. Our officers learned to do the long marches in the relative cool of the night. By autumn, we could reel off successive twenty milers and then, a day later, do speed marches covering ten miles in a bit over two hours.

The S-2 squad concentrated on sharpening its patrol skills, particularly those that would be useful at night. The length of my natural stride, for example, was measured time and time again, so that by counting the number of steps I took to cover a distance, I could give a fairly accurate estimate of how far I had moved, even in total darkness. That was in conjunction with learning to use a compass by the light of a cigarette lighter or flashlight and determining direction while under the cover of a raincoat to avoid detection. The proficiency test for that exercise was to maneuver, at night, over a patrol route consisting of directions written out like "go 200 yards at an azimuth of 187 degrees, then 70 yards at 330 degrees, then 167 yards at 87 degrees." The course was usually about a mile in length with eight to ten legs. It began and ended with stakes driven into the ground, and the measure of success was determined by how close to the ending stake a GI could finish. The individual members of our S-2 squad consistently arrived within a few feet of the finish marker. This indicated extraordinary skill.

We were also introduced to the combat course, using live ammo that tested our ability to advance on an "enemy," and shooting accurately with our combat arms. The "enemy" consisted of pop-up targets, controlled by officers safely hidden in the bunkers. I soon learned the most effective way to shoot while walking and stalking was by holding my rifle at the hip and firing to hit just in front of the target. The ricochet had a better chance of a hit than trying to make a "kill" by hitting the target directly. A wildly spinning, ricocheting bullet would also do more damage to skin and bone than the neat hole left by a rotating bullet. The aiming was done instinctively—just point and shoot—without using the sight. Firing from the prone or kneeling position was a different matter. There was time to aim using the sights. But while on the move forward toward expected enemy positions, there would rarely be time to get the weapon to shoulder height, aim, and fire while the enemy was firing at you.

WHILE WE TOOK this training with deadly seriousness, we were miffed that we had been plucked out of our cool alpine paradise in Colorado and sent to the hot, humid plains of Texas in the middle of a scorching summer. Griping increased, morale plummeted, and I heard some guys even went AWOL. For those of us who remained at Camp Swift, located on the outskirts of Bastrop, we also looked forward to our off-duty hours when we, just like mice when the cat is away, could play.

On those occasions when I could wangle a weekend pass to Austin or Houston, I jumped at the chance. I vowed to stay true to Lois back in Chicago, but I also missed the companionship of a soft, attractive female. You can only stand to be in the constant presence of other males for so long. This is when I made the acquaintance of two Texas ladies. I never contemplated them as more than just friends. Both of them were named Dottie.

Dottie in Austin:

Johnny had caught KP for one weekend so, on a Saturday after inspection, I headed for Austin. Transportation, by truck, was more like a cattle-car jaunt. Semi-trailers originally meant to haul small herds had a series of vertical poles erected at intervals inside the cavernous vehicles and for a pittance (a buck, I think), we were hauled the roughly thirty miles from camp to the USO in Austin.

A boarding house was located a few blocks east of downtown in a section of what had once been elegant housing circa World War I. The owner, a lady about my mother's age, furnished a screened-in porch, which reached across the width of the second floor, with a series of cots. These were rented to GIs for a dollar a night and included bathroom (but not shower) facilities. I made straight for the house and laid claim to one of the cots before heading to the USO. This involved just leaving my toilet kit on the bed. Perhaps not surprisingly, no one ever tried to pre-empt me by removing my kit.

At the USO, a dance was in progress. For some reason, there were more girls than men. I bellied up to the bar for a Coke and before long was approached by a pretty girl who said, "My name is Dottie. Would you like to dance?"

"Sure," I said, and in a moment we were moving easily to a Glenn Miller tune. We danced a few and sat out a few until the hour grew late. I asked if I could see her home. She hesitated, then acquiesced, and soon we boarded a bus. In uniform, I rode for free, and she dropped a dime in the meter for her fare. The bus crawled to the north side of Austin, and we disembarked. As we walked from the bus, Dottie explained that she was a sophomore co-ed at the University of Texas with no serious attachment.

When we reached her house, she invited me in to meet her family, who greeted me warmly. Her mother offered me iced tea and a piece of cake, and her father joined the conversation asking about the 10th and our training. Before long, I was asked to join the family for brunch after church in the morning. As midnight approached, I excused myself, walked back to the bus stop, and in a few minutes was back at the boarding house.

The next day I caught an early bus back to her neighborhood. After brunch, Dottie asked if I would like to go swimming. "Yes, but I have no bathing suit," was my response. Her dad offered his, and we headed for Austin's famous swimming hole at Barton Springs. We spent the afternoon mostly sunbathing because in those days (and since) I have not been fond of icy water. It was altogether a pleasant way to spend the weekend. I made sure I got Dottie's number and on Sunday evening headed back to the "cattle car" and the trip back to Camp Swift.

I related the weekend's adventures to Johnny as we lay on our cots, but his KP stint had filled him with sour grapes. He pretended I made the whole thing up and sent fake snores crashing against the wall to drown me out.

The following week I drew another weekend pass, and this time so did Johnny. I called Dottie to tell her I was coming in again and asked if she could find a date for Johnny. "It's vacation time," she explained, and her sorority sisters had all headed home for the summer. She agreed to meet us at the USO and suggested we go to the swimming hole again. This time I took a bathing suit.

Johnny and I checked in at the boarding house early on Saturday afternoon. We headed for the USO and were met there by a handful of our buddies who Johnny had tipped off. Well, six is a crowd, but Dottie and I took it in good spirits since neither of us wanted to get heavily involved anyway.

We met purely as friends a few more times over the summer. As fall approached and her scheduled classes began, we just kind of eased away from each other. I've often wondered what happened to her. Since I never recorded her last name, finding her would be difficult.

<u>Dottie in Houston:</u>

Early in November of 1944, Johnny and I took a weekend pass from Camp Swift and hopped the Katy Railroad to Houston. I had maybe ten dollars in my pocket, and we planned for a dollar-a-night cot in the ballroom of an elegant downtown Houston hotel. This was a "patriotic" gesture by the hotel whose rooms, we guessed, usually went for an unreachable (for us GIs) ten dollars a night. The ballroom was virtually unused in wartime, so army cots were lined up in never-ending rows. The several hundred lucky GI guests shared the john in the lobby, where no showers were available. Selflessly overcome by love of country and anxious to serve the soldiers, the hotel garnered a few hundred extra bucks every weekend night.

Johnny and I went directly to the hotel from the station and secured our weekend quarters. It was nearly 9 o'clock that night before we were ready for the next move. One of the guys had told us about *THE* hot spot to meet girls—the Chinese

Duck, located a few blocks from the downtown area.

Johnny and I wasted no time heading in that direction. You had to be twenty-one to buy a drink in Texas in those days, so at age nineteen we came well prepared with a forged note on the pass…ostensibly from Sergeant Leisentreit. He knew about these minor-league forgeries, but as long as we stayed out of trouble, he looked the other way.

The Chinese Duck was a barn of a place—a honky-tonk done in blue neon with a Chinese lantern theme setting the mood. A cloned Glenn Miller-type band played music of the era as Johnny and I found a table. We unhesitatingly ordered a rum and Coke and, through nearly impenetrable clouds of smoke, we simultaneously spotted two girls sitting a few tables away.

"The blonde's mine," Johnny announced. I had already decided that the other girl, a slender brunette, was more my style. We were up in a flash with invitations to dance.

"I'm Dottie," the brunette said as she slipped into my arms. We melted into the gloom, swaying to the music.

"I'm Marty," I answered, "and you're a terrific dancer."

"Not with everyone, but you're easy to follow and really smooth." She knew exactly what to say. It was like we were *ONE*, and with cheeks pressed tightly together, the two of us drifted around the floor in a dreamlike trance. Even when jitterbugs interspersed with the slow dances, we seemed to anticipate each other's every move. It was like discovering the mirror image of another self. When the dreamy music resumed, our bodies clung to each other.

Through the heavy cloth of my Eisenhower jacket, I could feel her breasts. My hand at her back couldn't discern the band of a bra, and I was soon convinced she wasn't wearing one. When the music stopped and we parted momentarily, I saw her nipples had risen to push through the cloth of her blouse. She noticed me staring, and even in the dim light I could see her blush.

Johnny and the blonde returned to the table, and I could sense that all was not well between them. They sat transfixed in mutual boredom over their drinks while Dottie and I held hands and chattered until the band started playing again. We were up in an instant and spent the next thirty minutes spinning through paradise again. Another session over another drink, and the conversation revealed that she was only sixteen, a high-school student living with her mother who worked the 4 p.m.-to-midnight shift at a war plant. Her father was not mentioned.

"Can we meet tomorrow?" I asked, and she immediately agreed.

"I have to be home tonight before my mom is, or she'll kill me. Tomorrow is Sunday, so let's meet for lunch. I'll make some sandwiches and we'll picnic in the park. Meet me at the USO at eleven."

By this time, the blonde had disappeared. Johnny sullenly bid us goodnight and headed back towards the hotel. Holding hands, Dottie and I sauntered out the door and walked a few blocks to a streetcar stop. In moments, a swaying, clanking streetcar arrived. Dottie leaned over, placed a gentle peck on my lips, and waved a smiling goodnight. A cynic would say that I had struck out.

An aging bellboy rousted us out of bed at 9 o'clock Sunday morning. While we waited in line for one of the sinks, I told Johnny about my plans for the day. "I'll see you back in camp," he grumbled. "I hate this town and particularly the women in it."

When we finished our cleanup, he waved goodbye and headed for the railroad station. He never did tell me what had happened between him and the blonde.

I strolled toward the USO and Dottie, half wondering if she'd really be there. She was, picnic basket and all. We had one of those idyllic days, suitable for a Jimmy Stewart movie. Warmed by a fall sun, comfortable even for Houston, we sat by a pond in the park and watched a parade of duck families. We wandered down meandering paths. We watched some kids playing touch football, and talked, and talked, and talked. Eventually, I told her I had a girl back home.

She hesitated for a few minutes and then blurted, "Couldn't we just be friends? Couldn't you just come back once in a while?"

By now we were approaching departure time for the last train back to Austin. She walked with me to the corner, where I would take a streetcar back to the railroad station. I explained to her that I would soon be bound for overseas. This was probably my last weekend pass.

"But write to me," I said. "We can be friends that way."

I scribbled my name and address on a small notebook she dug from her purse as the streetcar rumbled toward us. I handed it to her and she grabbed my head in her hands and planted a "more than sixteen-years-old" kiss on my lips.

"I will write," she promised, and turned and ran as I climbed into the streetcar.

She never did. And I never saw or heard from her again.

When the division Table of Organization was changed to increase our firepower, the 81mm mortar and the .30-caliber heavy machine-gun squads were pulled from HQ Company and expanded into full weapons companies. Many of my friends from basic training were made non-coms in the new H Company weapons platoons, while I suffered the indignity of remaining a PFC in the S-2 squad. That meant I was still to be mortified by the dreaded KP at least once a month. I hated peeling huge mounds of potatoes, washing stacks of greasy pots and pans, and loading primitive dishwashers with hundreds of plates from each meal. My salvation came by hook and by crook (and the conniving of Sergeant Tibor Mikes, to whom I had become a sort of ad hoc assistant squad leader).

Under the new TO, an opening for a Chemical Warfare Specialist arose. It meant attending Gas School for a week, learning how to detect if chemicals, such as the dreaded mustard or chlorine gases, were being used against us by the enemy and then spreading the alarm. Thus educated, I could still function with the Intelligence Squad, but as a corporal instead of a PFC. I would become, in fact, Tibor's assistant squad leader.

But Mel Johnson, the communications sergeant, had other ideas. He had in his platoon a "busted" regular Army sergeant named Hennessy, whom he wanted as his assistant. To settle the matter, Mel and Tibor agreed that both Hennessy and I would attend the school. The one with the highest final exam mark would get the two stripes.

In the first session of the school, we learned that the nose was the primary tool of gas detection. Both of us were heavy smokers and wouldn't be able to smell discharged gas if we were immersed in it, but we managed to memorize what each gas smelled like through the deadening effect of tobacco, and what to do about it. We took the final exam. I answered all but two of the routine questions on the exam. A few days later I was astonished to learn that I had scored 100% versus only 98% for Hennessy. I was immediately awarded my stripes.

Knowing that I had not completed the test and could not have earned 100%, I was consumed with a guilty conscience and confessed to Tibor that I should not have been promoted. Tibor, hissing through clenched teeth, told me to shut my mouth, that my winning score had cost him some heavy-duty favors from the teaching non-com involved, and that I should not question anyone further. Thus, I never did another stint at KP.

Late in the fall, with our morale at its very lowest, we got a new commanding general, George P. Hays, who had been awarded the Medal of Honor for his actions in World War I. Our collective confidence and morale was lifted when among his first actions, he told us that our name had been changed from the "10th Light Division (Alpine, Pack)" to the "10th Mountain Division" and we were issued small "Mountain" tabs to sew above the crossed-bayonet sleeve insignia.

Deployment rumors started again. By mid-December, we were packing for another division-sized move. As we boarded the trains for Camp Patrick Henry, Virginia, in late December we learned about the Germans' massive surprise attack in the Ardennes that soon became known as "The Battle of the Bulge." We were convinced that we were Belgium-bound.

We arrived at the POE (Port of Embarkation) around Christmas time in blustery cold and depressing weather. We were re-issued clean uniforms, were administered a fresh slew of medical shots, and did a bit of training on the cargo nets in case we had to debark from a slowly sinking troop ship. Our Christmas entertainment was provided by a newly inducted soldier named Red Skelton. We were permitted to attend movies or get high on 4.2% beer every night.

During my final shower at Camp Patrick Henry, I hung my dog tags over the showerhead, and forgot to retrieve them. They somehow disappeared. I immediately requested another pair, which did not catch up to me until I was about to be discharged more than a year later. I could easily have been just another "unknown soldier" had I been KIA (killed in action).

Finally, with all our gear loaded in the barracks bags, we entrained to the dock at the huge naval base at Newport News, Virginia, and found a mammoth ocean liner awaiting us. We shouldered our bags and rifles and shuffled in long lines to the gangplank. As we reached it, an officer armed with a clipboard called out our names, to which we responded with our serial numbers. We then staggered up the gangplank to the deck and were led down endless steps to a cavernous room on a lower deck. This was to be our accommodations on the troop ship USS *West Point* (formerly the luxury liner, *America*). It wasn't until we were all at sea that our destination was announced: Naples, Italy.

The long hours on the ship gave few choices of how to pass the time. Exploring through unmarked passages led me to a few quiet zones, where I could sit quietly and sneak a cigarette even when the "smoking lamp" was not lit.

# 12:
# The Voyage to Perdition

I learned after the war that the 10th had a reputation as a bunch of playboys, and maybe it was true. Many of the guys in the division had come from wealthy, East Coast families, where skiing was a rich man's sport (lift tickets were $2.00 a day!). A goodly number were on the ski teams at the Ivy League schools, and some were even Olympic skiers. Many of the cadre and instructors were foreign-born skiers from occupied Norway, Austria, and even Germany who decided they didn't want to fight for Hitler. Some of them, like Walter Prager, the Dartmouth ski team coach, were from Switzerland.

Because of all the college-educated athletes and "blue bloods" in the division, and the cockiness that went with it, the 10th seemed to be constantly featured in magazines, newspapers, radio programs, and even the movies. Maybe so much attention was focused on us because, by the end of 1944, we were just about the last Army division stateside; the rest had already been shipped out to the combat zones.

Most of the guys in the 10th were itching to go overseas. After all, we hadn't joined up just to stay home while the other outfits were in the thick of the fighting. We wanted to see action. But there were a couple of problems. One was that we were a "mountain" division, and the Army was looking for some mountainous place where our skills could be put to the best advantage. And two, we had about 5,000 pack mules and horses. They caused a big logistics problem—how do you feed, stable, transport, and care for 5,000 mules and horses, especially at a time when the Army had all but switched from animals to motors?

But General Mark Clark in Italy was in trouble. His units there were still fighting and dying for yards of real estate in the rugged mountains of Italy, the Apennines. Just a handful of Germans holding the high ground could stop an entire division struggling along on a narrow mountain road. When Clark found out that we—a division specially trained for mountain warfare—were still in the States, he immediately requested that we be sent over. And we were.

THE USS *AMERICA* once had been the queen of the United States' luxury fleet, but now she had been stripped of every amenity. This was the military's "sardine can" theory of packing as many troops as possible into her hull. Now the USS *West Point*, sections of her hold contained steel bunks six tiers high into which thousands of men were crammed with their equipment. Every square foot of available space was used to house troops.

The open walkways along the deck were boarded over to provide barracks for additional soldiers. A few days out in the heavy seas, a winter storm shattered the plywood walls and washed away the equipment and clothing of dozens of men.

The public rooms were converted into huge mess halls. Long lines filled the corridors before every meal. The joke of the day was a cartoon showing the skeleton of a deceased soldier who died waiting to reach the mess hall. We filed in twice a day, clutching our mess kits into which hot meals were plopped unceremoniously. Lunch consisted of K-rations. Gang showers were cold salt-water sprays, and we were cautioned not to over-use the limited supply of drinking water. The ship was thought to be fast enough to outrun any German U-boat and ran the route across the Atlantic at top speed.

Craps games filled the boring hours. The winners of each were invited to participate in playoffs, with a single winner for the whole ship emerging. It was rumored that the winner had amassed tens of thousands of dollars, which the ship's captain wired home. I had only ten dollars with me and managed to lose it all on my first pass of the dice. So much for my gambling luck.

The only other diversion was the occasional target practice that Navy gun crews took with their five-inch guns. As huge as the ship was, the recoil and noise of those pieces vibrated and shook every steel plate on the vessel. We had no escort of any kind while crossing, but I guess we were safe enough, given our speed and armament. We could out-run or out-gun any sub afloat—unless they got lucky with a torpedo.

We had left the U.S. on January 3, 1945, and after nearly a week at sea we passed the Rock of Gibraltar, confirming our destination to be the Mediterranean. Soon, we steamed slowly into the chaos of Naples Harbor and docked next to a much smaller British troop ship. We kidded the Tommies about their puny ship, but they had the perfect response: "This is just a lifeboat off the *Queen Mary*, Yank!"

Naples' docks were evidence of the devastation caused by the Germans. Dozens of sunken and overturned ships lined the harbor, but American ingenuity used them as foundations for new piers. Engineers had constructed walkways, roads, and ramps on top of the half-submerged hulls, and unloading proceeded apace.

The harbor area was crowded with hordes of rag-clad children and adults begging for food, and they lined up clasping #10 cans with wire handles to hold everything we offered. We were forbidden to give our rations to them, and the ship's PX soon ran out of candy and snacks which we purchased in their behalf. My very first "letter to the editor," published by the *Christian Science Monitor*, described the devastation and poverty.

In a day or two, our company disembarked and was transferred to a LCI (Landing Craft Infantry) that slipped away at night and headed north along the western coast of Italy. Compared to the *West Point*, the LCI was an experience in misery. The unventilated below-deck facilities stunk of human sweat and drove most of the men to seek some small huddle-space on the top deck. The only food was provided by K-rations, supplemented with putrid coffee. Sanitary facilities consisted of stools that emptied directly into the sea and were cordoned off by flapping canvas partitions. The only drinking water was what we had brought aboard in canteens.

Daylight brought a more pleasant environment. A warm winter sun took the night's chill from our bones as we cruised along the beautiful Italian coast to Leghorn (also known as Livorno). A line of trucks at the dock awaited us, and after a brief ride we were disgorged onto a huge field at the edge of which the famed Leaning Tower of Pisa could be seen. Rows of perfectly aligned pup tents were erected in which we lived while we removed gobs of cosmoline from our weapons and equipment. Cosmoline was grease distilled to an almost tar-like consistency and was applied to prevent the ocean's salt air from forming rust on the steel. It took hours of applying sufficient solvent and elbow grease to remove it and get the weapons in operating condition.

Despite our tents being aligned like a peacetime garrison encampment, we were warned that we were in a war environment. We were told of a tragic incident that occurred a few days prior to our arrival when some of the 86th Mountain Infantry Regiment men, who had preceded us at the campground, wandered down an adjacent railroad track and into a booby-trapped area. Several men were killed, including medics and a chaplain who sprang to their aid. Thereafter, we watched carefully where we walked.

OUR TRIP FROM Pisa up to the front lines was without incident; the Germans–or "krauts" and "Jerries" as we called them—had pulled northward, into the last line of mountains before the land flattens out into the rich and fertile Po River Valley. On January 17, 1945, I wrote to Lois and gave her my impressions of what I'd seen

The 10th's route of march—from Naples, into the northern Apennine Mountains, and on to Lake Garda—January-May 1945

thus far: *"Jerry is a tenacious fighter, which leaves a very visible imprint on the towns. Whole communities are laid completely to waste—what used to be a town is now a gigantic heap of rubble."*

In another letter, written a few days later, I wrote, *"Crazy as it may sound, I'm almost anxious to get in a hot spot, out of the simple curiosity of wondering how I'll react. I'd like to prove to myself whether or not I can take it."*

Needless to say, Lois was not pleased with my telling her of my desire to "get in a hot spot."

AFTER A DAY or so, I was pulled aside along with a section of the communications platoon. We were told to pack all our gear and were hustled to a waiting six-by-six truck. We spent the next few hours following winding mountain roads, passing rubble-strewn hamlets and a wrecked power plant at a town named Pistoia.

We arrived in the dark at the edge of a tiny mountain town named Gavinanna. This would be the headquarters of 2nd Battalion, 85th Mountain Infantry Regiment. It was now occupied by a small group of men from the 86th Mountain Infantry, who were generous in sharing their rations. Several of them were medics, who rattled us a bit with tales of being fired upon as they attempted to treat and rescue wounded patrol members. Rather than giving the protection mandated by the Geneva Convention, the red crosses painted on their helmets made them targets for German snipers. One of the medics showed me a captured Beretta pistol he now unobtrusively carried for self-protection, also in violation of the Geneva Convention.

The building that would house HQ Company had been a tuberculosis sanitarium at the eastern edge of town. All the furniture was removed, but I was instructed by the accompanying officer to plot the location for each HQ platoon within the building and give them billeting assignments as they arrived over the next few days. I was also designated as Sergeant of Guard, despite my inferior rank as a corporal, and was told to plan the defense of the building.

The Germans were several miles to the north, beyond the mountain shoulder against which the town huddled. I explored the area around the building and arranged for outposts and listening posts in an arc a hundred yards or so uphill from our position. I placed another outpost at the entrance of the circular driveway of the road that led to our unit. Each position was to be manned by the men from one of the HQ platoons—anti-tank, ammunition and pioneering, communications, and S-2—in two-hour shifts. That drew the loudest protests from my S-2 squad, which, as the smallest group, had only six PFCs and therefore would be on guard duty every single night. To compensate, I gave them the easiest post at the front of the building, which had sort of a guard shack for shelter from the weather. The others used foxholes dug by the previous occupants. We hadn't yet received enough wire to establish telephone communication between the outposts and the HQ building, so we agreed to rely on shouting a warning or firing shots to spread any alarms.

It didn't take long to get the first test of our defense system. One night I was sitting in my cubicle when a shot rang out from the north side of our quarters. I grabbed my M-1 and, yelling the alarm, ran outside to help repel the attack. In the semi-darkness I found Fearless Fosberg with his arm around the enemy, who turned out to be one of our own men. He had wandered out back on a toilet mission, and was returning when challenged for the password, which he had forgotten. Fearless had then let a round from his carbine fly, barely missing the soldier. The one round in the chamber had fired, but he had inadvertently pressed the clip release instead of the safety. The clip fell to the ground, so a second bullet never entered the chamber of his semi-automatic carbine. The firing pin had clicked, instead, on an empty chamber. Lucky us. The near miss had saved us from a friendly-fire casualty.

## 13:
## First Action

For the remainder of January and into early February of 1945, we stayed relatively idle. Johnny and Ned were pulled from the squad to man an outpost in a farmhouse a mile or so above us and were given walkie-talkies for maintaining contact. The farmer there treated the two men as family. Even though they alternated two hours on, two hours off continuously for twenty-four-hour shifts, both of my friends almost enjoyed the duty.

I was ordered to guide a special detail. We were supposed to establish an outpost along a high ridge overlooking the town of Cutigliano, to the west of our position. The ridge was situated along an easy route for infiltration by the enemy onto the road leading to the town of Bagni di Lucca. The outpost was to be manned on a rotating basis by a few men from a line company squad. Aerial photos indicated that a shepherd's hut straddled the ridgeline. It would give the outpost some shelter against the still frigid and snowy weather. The outpost would be connected by telephone to its company HQ. The few men manning the post would be no match for a marauding German patrol or infiltration but could raise a warning in time to get an opposing force into a defensive position close to the town.

Lieutenant David W., the communications officer, commanded the detail. Fearless Fosberg, accompanied by several of his wiremen, laid the telephone line the two miles or so up the mountain. As the only trained scout in the detail, I was to locate the hut whose position I had marked on a 1/25,000-scale map and lead the way. I had to make sure the area was clear of enemy troops before leading the party to the ridge top. The two men from the line company, who would initially man the outpost, would provide what additional firepower might be needed if we ran into trouble. The climb, through deep snow without benefit of skis or snowshoes, took several hours. Lieutenant W. stayed below to "protect the vehicles."

When we reached the edge of the tree line, I carefully scoped the scene and could not pick up any sign of activity or movement at the ridge top. Leading the two riflemen, I waded through the drifts toward the hut, noting that there were no other footprints or paths through the nearby snowdrifts. I approached the door to the half-buried shack and, holding my M-1 at the ready, kicked in the door. The building was empty. Inside, there was a single chair, a small table, and a straw-covered pallet that served as a bed—just enough room for the two-man shifts that would now occupy the building. I checked carefully for any trip wires and booby traps, and found none.

After installing and testing the telephone, we left the two riflemen and began the mountain descent through deep drifts. About halfway down we were subjected to a very long-range machine-gun fire from German positions to our north. We all took off running downhill at breakneck speed until a neighboring ridge sheltered us from observation. This was my first episode of being under enemy fire and earned me the Combat Infantry Badge. Big deal. Most important to me was the extra ten bucks a month combat pay the CIB brought.

The days at Gavinanna were too easy to last long. After not bathing for a week, we were told to leave our wallets and personal items in our barracks bags and were transported to a nearby town where a shower tent had been erected. Stripped of our uniforms, we were herded in long lines under a series of perforated pipes which spewed water heated to a point barely above freezing, given a minuscule bar of soap, and told to scrub down. Shivering, we were handed pitifully small towels and dried off. Then we ran through a supply line and, except for combat boots, were issued new uniforms. The hassle of paying a local *signora* a pack of cigarettes to sew on the 10th Mountain Division patch and my stripes came later.

The first sergeant took pity on us a week later and located a company laundress to wash and iron our clothes. Again, cigarettes were the medium of exchange. He also "borrowed" a submersible gasoline-powered water heater from the kitchen, and we used it to warm up enough water to take individual full-blown baths. The bathtubs in the sanitarium were carved from exquisite marble, but a supply of running water was not yet available for the town. All of our water was brought by truck in five-gallon cans. The problem may not have been a lack of water sources but the lack of electricity to power the town pumps.

Personal hygiene became easier by virtue of the value of cigarettes. A few handed to the town barber solved the daily shaving problem. The shaving cream came from the PX, but the barber was an artist with a keenly honed straight razor, much like the one my father had used for years. A pack of even a third-rate brand of cigarettes like Fleetwood took care of a full week's laundry, returned clean and lovingly ironed with creases in all the right places. For those so inclined, a full carton would buy the attention of a pretty *signorina*, who came minus an anti-disease warranty.

The tracked weasel, the mainstay of our field transportation, did a disappearing act. I don't recall ever seeing one once we arrived in Italy. The vehicles of choice were the jeep and the slightly bigger and more powerful weapons carrier. They were

both jealously guarded by those authorized to have one. The protection against theft was a stout chain fastened with a heavy lock running from the sharply turned steering wheel to a cleat on the jeep's side. At night, an extra precaution was to remove the rotor from the distributor.

Nicknames for the jeeps were commonly assigned. The funniest one I remember was for a jeep assigned to the company commander of one of our line companies. His driver named it *Umbriago*, which means drunkard. A humorless chaplain complained, and the brass made him remove the sign from the outside of the cowling.

The battalion's line companies were billeted in Gavinanna and little villages nearby connected by roads exposed to enemy infiltration for long stretches. Patrols of jeeps along these roads were established. The rifle companies bore responsibility to maintain those contacts, but often one man from the S-2 squad was sent along just to keep a hand in the activity.

Most of the time our day consisted of one boring hour after another, which gave me lots of time to read Lois' letters, which arrived in spurts, and for me to write back. At one point the censor (all outgoing mail was read by a censor to make sure it didn't contain any real news that might be of value to the enemy, should the enemy manage to intercept it) complained that I was sending "too many letters."

THE WEATHER WAS too miserable for even the German mountain troops. If they infiltrated at all, it went undetected by our patrols. Of course, the jeeps had no heaters and, under combat conditions, the windshield had to be folded down on the vehicle's hood and covered with canvas to avoid reflecting glare. The patrols during inclement weather were pure misery.

The Germans had devised an abhorrent method of attacking a jeep's occupants. When they could infiltrate, they would string a nearly invisible wire across the road, stretching from trees on opposite sides, just about neck high on a seated jeep driver and passenger. If the jeep's crew was unmindful of the danger, particularly at night, and sped merrily along, they could encounter the wire and immediately be decapitated. The countering strategy was to weld a vertical bar on the front bumper, which had a large notch with sharpened edges near its top end. If a speeding jeep encountered a wire, it would slide up the bar into the notch and be cut and rendered harmless.

I participated in a few other missions in early February. Bob Fels, the battalion S-3 (Operations) sergeant, and I were bundled into a jeep with all of our worldly possessions stashed in a trailer and hustled under mysterious secrecy westward to the town of Bagni di Lucca, north of Leghorn/Livorno. Once there, we were

dropped off at a magnificent in-town villa. We later learned it was the summer home of an Italian doctor and his college-age son, Pietro. The house was exquisitely furnished. I remember an elaborate stove standing in the living room as a heating source. Unfortunately, there was neither coal nor wood available, so despite its beauty, the stove was small comfort. I did get the luxury of a bedroom—complete with feather mattress and comforter—all to myself. I was permitted to use it only during daylight hours. At night I slept on a cot angled in front of the door to a downstairs front room to prevent entry to where Bob Fels performed his secret mission. It was off limits to everyone except himself and the operations officer, who made infrequent visits over the next few days.

My curiosity about what was going on in there was driving me nuts. It wasn't until our last day there that Bob let me see the room, and then only because he needed me to help carry his handiwork to a waiting truck.

His project had been a detailed clay model of a mountain range, which had a small sign indentifying it as "Belvedere." The model occupied all of a plywood base about four feet square and was obviously intended as a tool to brief our officers and acquaint them with the terrain over which we would soon launch an attack. Our secret location for the project was to minimize any chance that information about the locale would be compromised.

We carefully covered the model with blankets, loaded it into the back of a truck, and returned to Gavinanna, sneaking it into a room at our HQ. The room was then locked. I located the mountain on one of my maps but kept my mouth shut about the whole affair. Even when pressed by Tibor, my S-2 sergeant, I wouldn't reveal the secret.

A FEW DAYS later, Jessie, the S-2 officer, shook me awake before dawn and handed me an extra bandoleer of ammo for my M-1. With no explanation of where we were headed, together with Lieutenant Colonel John S., our battalion commander, we rode in a blacked-out jeep to a little town named Lizzano. It was still dark when we arrived, and the driver parked the jeep behind a barn to deny the Germans any knowledge of our presence. The buildings were occupied by GIs who were forbidden to stray outside lest their presence be observed by German outposts. Several other officers joined our group.

In the gray dawn, maintaining wide separation, we picked our way over the grassy no-man's land to an outpost occupied by the division-size Brazilian Expeditionary Force, part of the multi-national Fifth Army. Beyond them lay the German positions. Led by a few Brazilians, who soon dropped back after pointing out a gently rising knoll behind which we were to make our approach, the officers crawled

Riva Ridge—the enemy-held series of connected peaks that the 10th Mountain Division climbed on the night of February 18/19, 1945

(U.S. Army photo)

assembled and, as a group, were asked to express by a show of hands how they felt about the competence of our officers. We voted on them one by one. When we got to S., only one butt-kissing private indicated confidence in S.'s leadership capabilities. More than 100 men gave him thumbs-down.

In fairness, a weapons-company machine-gun sergeant later told me that he witnessed the lieutenant colonel, under shellfire and at great person risk, trying to rally men out of the woods on the ridge. They paid him no heed. Perhaps he had great courage but failed as a leader and motivator. I tried in vain to reach him in postwar years, but he did not respond to my letter.

Another memorable officer was Lieutenant David W. He was an easy-going, personally likeable chap, but he managed to evade risk whenever it posed a possible threat to him. When his communications platoon was assigned any job that included risk, without fail he handed that job off to Sergeant Johnson or some other non-com. He then stayed far enough back to minimize his own danger but still observe what was happening.

He was so likeable that Lois and I welcomed him and his female companion (Lucy, I think) when they came through Dallas postwar on a cross-country motorcycle trip. He regaled us with stories of his international jaunts on an Italian motorcycle that he finagled by promises of publicity to its manufacturer.

"Big f—— operator" would be a suitable appellation.

THE HUGE SEARCHLIGHTS, positioned on the hills behind us, sent up beams that bounced off the clouds, creating artificial moonlight and also serving to blind the Germans. As the company and the rest of the 2nd Battalion silently filed into the heavy timber, I pointed out the areas to which I assigned each of the HQ sections and—as quietly as the rock soil would permit—they dug in, forming a defensive perimeter. We were to be the reserve battalion, hidden right behind the 3rd Battalion, which would launch its attack on Belvedere without benefit of artillery preparation. Lieutenant James, shovel in hand, came to me as I was digging in.

"Colonel S. needs a foxhole," he said, handing me the shovel, hinting that it was my next chore. That was the ultimate "no-no" request for a field officer to make. Every man is expected to dig his own protection. Lieutenant Colonel S. was no exception. James returned within minutes and said, "Forget it. Dig your own." I think he was embarrassed by S.'s request. The shovel he left was a much better tool for me to dig my own foxhole.

# 14: Belvedere

In the dark of night on February 19, the 1st and 3rd Battalions of the 85th jumped off toward Monte Belvedere and its adjacent peak, Monte Gorgolesco, as planned. They were forbidden to have ammo in their weapons because the flash of their shots would reveal their positions. Any gunshot flashes would be presumed to be from the Germans, who were to be attacked with grenades and bayonets.

Back at our command post, we could hear the stutter of German machine guns, the *karumph* of their mortars, and the crack of their 88s as they sought to stop the advance. The attack continued through the night. By dawn on February 20, the peaks were in our hands, and the enemy's counterattacks began. We began the move to the top of the saddle.

Dead American and German soldiers lying in the snow on Mt. Belvedere, February 19, 1945. Riva Ridge is visible in the background.

(U.S. Army photo)

Our battalion had been committed to the attack in late afternoon. The rest of the S-2 squad was ahead with the line companies, gathering intelligence for the battalion commander, Lieutenant Colonel S. In a line of companies, the battalion was strung out halfway along the peaks and saddles reaching toward the next division objective, Monte Della Torraccia, three miles to the northeast.

I had just finished leveling off the bottom of a shallow trench in which to grab a little shut-eye when Shep arrived. He couldn't stand being at the command post when all the action was further up the ridge. "Daneman, do you want to take a little walk?"

It must have been nearly midnight when we started our silent trek across the slopes. Darkness falls deeply in the Italian winter. The huge anti-aircraft spotlights ranging along peaks to our south sent their beams bouncing off the winter haze, creating the artificial moonlight by which we made our way. Neither of us spoke. Only the rustle of our gear and the squeaky crunch of our mountain boots penetrating the frozen shell on the snow broke the silence. A half-mile gap extended between our battalion and the main line of the division. We stole through the trees just under the undulating crest of the tree line, wary of bypassed Krauts or their probing patrols. They still held the lower reaches north and west of the peaks, and a wrong turn would put us in their midst. With only sidelong glances, we passed some of the anonymous dead, sprawled grotesquely, silhouetted against the snow.

Suddenly, a low moan drifted from an isolated clump of artillery-felled trees. With rifles leveled, we stealthily approached the fallen timber and stumbled over a wounded GI, half hidden under a log. A bloody "M" was painted on his forehead, indicating he'd already received a shot of morphine. No continuous bleeding was apparent, so we covered him with blankets as best we could, and with the promise to send aid, we pushed on.

Finally, beyond the ruins of a tiny mountain church, Cappel di Ronchidas, on a ridge of towering chestnut trees, we stumbled on a cluster of foxholes. Muffled voices answered our password, and whispered directions sent us further into the defense perimeter to the log-covered dugout which sheltered the 2nd Battalion's advance command post. Inside, by the flickering yellow beams of a candle, we found Lieutenant Colonel S. huddled over a map. Whispered animated conversation with a handful of line company officers was punctuated by agonized whimperings of pain.

Three or four wounded men, eyes glazed over with morphine, lay prone along the dugout's floor. In the semi-darkness, it was difficult to discern between the sleep of exhaustion and the immobility of pain. As I noticed the soldiers, I worried about Johnny and Ned, my close friends who had been dispatched to an observation outpost somewhere nearby.

Suddenly the shelling, which had been intermittent, intensified.

The Germans were zeroed in on the dugout they had built and correctly surmised that we would also use. A relentless rain of shells split the earth. The ground trembled, and granules from the rent bags poured between the logs that formed the ceiling. The noise was ear-shattering; even hands cupped over the ears could not relieve the pain of concussion.

Outside, the men who cowered in frantically dug foxholes began taking hits from overhead artillery and mortar tree-bursts. The illusionary shelter of the chestnut trees instead became an umbrella of death.

Some of the wounded who could still crawl headed for the dugout and soon it was crammed with men. *This isn't for me*, I thought. One lucky direct hit would have collapsed the roof and annihilated all of us. I searched for Shep but, in the sea of helmets, I couldn't pick him out. Crawling over and under the seething bodies, I slowly squeezed to the exit.

During a brief lull in the shelling, I dashed from the dugout and toward a narrow, windswept gulley outlined by a snow-covered clearing. The crescendo of crashing shell bursts persisted. For what seemed like hours I pressed my face and body into the cold snow, not daring to move. Shrieking chunks of shrapnel tore through the air inches over my head, slashing huge holes in the tree trunks and sending them crashing to the ground. Nearby, pain-filled cries of "Medic" and "Mama" punctuated the screams of the wounded.

From somewhere along the ridge came a cry that ricocheted from the peaks: "*HERE THEY COME!!!*"

The German counter-attack had begun. A deep-seated voice boomed in my head: "These guys, my buddies, need me," drowning out a nearly silent voice of reason telling me to "get the hell out of here."

Leaving the safety of the gulley, I threaded my way through the fallen timber on a trail past a dozen ravaged bodies. Captain Bennett, the CO of H Company, his face and head rent by a huge shrapnel tear, sprawled dead along with several others in a half-completed trench. I soon found myself amongst what was left of a G Company rifle platoon. They huddled in a crooked row of foxholes, rifles pointed toward a pasture at the edge of the woods a few yards ahead. I reached to the back of my pistol belt for my shovel to dig in; it was gone. My bayonet and scabbard hung by a single hook, the other cleanly snipped off. Had shrapnel scythed across the equipment on my back, leaving me unscathed?

I tossed the scabbard away and slipped the bayonet over the barrel and stud of my M-1 rifle. A nearby GI watched me, clicked his own bayonet into position, and "Fix bayonets," echoed across the mountain. I borrowed an entrenching tool from the unmoving body of a GI and began enlarging the foxhole that had failed to protect him.

With the addition of a barricade of fallen trees providing a makeshift redoubt, I poked my rifle barrel toward German positions across the clearing. In a moment, a chorus of rifle and automatic weapons began their staccato song. The timpani joined in as our 60mm mortars entered the fray. Fifty yards or so down the ridge, ahead of our lines, a fleeting figure in gray crossed an opening in the trees, and I let a round fly. I don't think I hit him; at least I didn't see him go down, but it felt good to be firing back.

The hours spent huddled and defenseless under German shellfire had left me trembling with rage and frustration. Soon, the firing became desultory and, as targets disappeared, "Cease fire" rang out from somewhere down the line. The German counter-attack had fizzled out.

I joined in as the platoon dug into their pockets for a belated K-ration breakfast. When it appeared that more than a momentary lull had developed, I worked my way back along the crest, pausing to help evacuate some wounded to the aid station at Ronchidas. Shep crossed my mind. I scouted around the now-empty dugout, not knowing whether he had made it out or was among the myriad of bodies that lay twisted, prone, and half-buried in the carnage. I believed there was no way he could have been as lucky as me.

As I stumbled with fatigue back along the ridge toward our jumping-off place, I tried to be aware of the as-yet-uncleared mines, walking only where previous feet had trod. Stan Nelson, a company communications lineman out to repair our shredded telephone network, shocked me with the news that Johnny and Ned, my two closest friends since our basic training days, had taken a direct hit in their observation post foxhole and were dead. Numb with disbelieving shock, grief, and fatigue, and no longer caring about the uncleared mines or bypassed German troops, I staggered back to the company command post, and the S-2 sergeant.

"Tibor," I cried in anguish. "They're dead. Johnny and Ned are dead." And then I choked out, "Maybe Shep is, too."

Tibor's shoulders sagged with the news. They were his friends, too. He had alternately coddled them and relentlessly driven them until, according to the division's Readiness tests, their squad—our squad—had become the best scouts in his regiment. His head shaking in disbelief, he muttered, "No, no, no. It can't be."

Just then, a figure loomed over the ridge, his face concealed by the sun at his back. A moment later, almost in a torpor, Shep came into the CP. "My God, Daneman. I thought you had bought it. I looked all over that ridge for you."

"Captain, that goes double for me," was my hoarse but joyous reply. Then, some eighteen hours late, I staggered toward my slit trench to fitfully begin my rest. Torn between anguish and exhaustion, sleep soon stilled my tears.

# 15: Johnny and Ned, the Aftermath

**February 22, 1945:**

My recollection of events over the next few days is disjointed and confusing. The shock of battle, the loss of my friends, and the horrors I witnessed took their toll. I remember the events but cannot break out of the fog to place an exact time-frame on any of them.

I was awakened at dawn by a distant barrage. The cooks had risked the mine-fields and set up a field kitchen nearby. I washed down the hot breakfast of watery eggs and limp, greasy bacon with a canteen of something resembling coffee. Every-thing was tasteless.

Tibor pointed down the hill to the road that had been our line of departure and told us to assemble there and await the trucks that would take us to a new command post. As I reached the road, a truck rumbled by carrying some of the walking wounded. I gasped as I saw Harry Weinsaft standing next to the tailgate and called out, "Harry, what happened?"

"I can't see," he responded. "I heard about Johnny and now I can't see." His voice faded as the truck drew away.

In a few minutes another truck pulled up and, together with Sergeant Leisentreit and a few other HQ Company men, I climbed aboard. We drove for less than an hour to the town of Gaggio Montano, then wended our way on a primitive dirt track halfway up the side of the ridge where our battalion was still heavily engaged and taking more casualties from the German barrages. We halted at a little group of houses that my map identified as Ronchidos di Sopra, less than a half-mile from the crest of the ridge.

"This is our new CP," Sergeant Leisentreit announced. "Marty, set up a defensive perimeter."

We had only a handful of men with us, but I positioned a few between us and where I assumed the Germans might be and dug a foxhole for myself next to a huge haystack. The hay looked much more inviting than the dirt, so I burrowed my way into the stack for a nap. In my exhaustion, the nap lasted all through the afternoon and all through the night.

The long sleep in the haystack restored my appetite. I caught up on my eating schedule by finishing both a breakfast and lunch of K-rations at once.

His sight restored, perhaps aided by the furious need to avenge his friends, Harry Weinsaft returned to the company. He was immediately put to work as an interpreter and began questioning German prisoners. I watched dispassionately from a few feet away as he tried to elicit information about their units with translated answers relayed for the benefit of the S-2 squad. The Germans, not sensing the cold anger seething in Harry, hesitated to give more than the customary "name, rank, and serial number."

Harry minced no words. He announced that he was a Jew (*Ich ben Juden*), his family had been murdered by the Nazis, two of his best friends had just died in battle, and unless his questions were answered immediately, he would cut off their balls

Me (left) and two of my best friends in the S-2 squad, Stan Nelson and Dave Williams

(U.S. Army photo)

and shove them up their noses. To give credence to his threat, Harry pulled out his trench knife from its scabbard and held it threateningly against the crotch of a prisoner. On his knees, the German pleaded for mercy. I restrained Harry as Lieutenant James, playing "good guy" to Harry's "bad guy," offered them cigarettes.

They had just begun to talk when Stan Nelson appeared around the corner of the farmhouse. Stan became Johnny's replacement on the S-2 squad. Dave Williams replaced Ned. Pete Cantine would fill in for Curly Lambert, who had been savaged in the same shelling. Curley survived, I don't know how. I saw him briefly, laid out on a stretcher, awaiting evacuation. I heard later that he had over a hundred shrapnel wounds.

"I found them, together in a foxhole, about a hundred yards from the church," Stan said.

He meant Johnny and Ned.

"By tomorrow that hill will be crawling with ghouls stealing their wallets and shoes," Stan said. "Let's get Johnny and Ned outta there."

"Too late today," I answered as I looked at the darkening sky. "I don't want to be crawling through a minefield in the dark. Let's do it at dawn tomorrow."

At sun up, Stan and I picked up a couple of mattress covers to use as body bags and edged up the trail to the summit. A Sherman tank, the left track shattered by a mine, sat a hundred yards or so up the trail. Its crew lounged nearby, not rushing to make the repairs that would have put them back in the battle.

"There's some unmarked *Schu* mines up there, so watch it," one of them warned.

"Thanks," we grunted. The lack of yellow tape to mark a cleared safe lane emphasized their warning.

Heads down, watching for the mines' telltale prongs, Stan and I made our way slowly to the ridge and the sheltering wreckage of what had been tall chestnut trees. Foxholes in a crazy-quilt pattern were everywhere, partly hidden by a tangle of fallen limbs from the shattered trees. Stan lined himself up between two knolls, angled off a few yards through the woods, and beckoned me over.

They lay half crouched, arm in arm, in a single foxhole. Johnny's helmet was askew but still on his head. The familiar jaw was clenched, and unseeing eyes stared through his glasses at the back of Ned's bare head. I closed his eyes with my fingers as rage-driven tears began to stream down my cheeks.

Stan and I struggled to separate the swollen bodies and lift them out of the foxhole. They were locked together in rigor mortis. With almost superhuman effort, we pulled them out of the hole and laid them side-by-side. We retrieved their wallets and one of their dog tags, struggling to get them into the mattress covers. Bloated by death, they would not fit. Calloused by necessity, in an act that haunts me to this day, I plunged my bayonet into each one and released the death-induced gas. Their bodies deflated like grotesque balloons. We managed to pull the mattress covers over them. Now sobbing, Stan and I finished the gruesome job. Tear-streaked, we made our way back to the CP.

Sergeant Leisentreit silently nodded as we handed the wallets and dog tags to him. "You shouldn't have done it, but I know how much they meant to you," he said after a moment. "I'll take care of it."

Stan and I walked over to the haystack and, each in his own thoughts, smoked a cigarette.

That night the battalion was withdrawn for a few days' rest, and to reorganize for the next battle.

UP TO NOW, my letters to Lois had maintained the charade that I was in a nice, safe, and boring spot, with little or no combat going on around me. I saw no reason to upset her or change the status quo now. On February 25, I wrote, *"It's been over a week since I last was able to write to you.... I can't say what I've been doing except that it was impossible for me to do any writing at all. Don't get any false ideas that I was in any danger or anything like that—it would just be your imagination working overtime again. I was just too busy to write, and let it go at that."*

All the while, however, the deaths of Johnny and Ned were eating away at me, and I had no one with whom I could unburden my grief. It wasn't until March 9 that I finally confessed to Lois that I had been withholding information from her: *"I've been keeping something from you and I think that I'd better tell you for several reasons.... I think you must have read in the papers about the attack on Mt. Belvedere, Mt. Della Torrachia [sic], etc. I was in on it, darling, and the story I'll tell you about it isn't pretty. There are still some things I can't say—not for a while yet, but I'll tell you what I can....*

*"I spotted one kraut running across a gully I was covering and shot him. I'd always wondered how I'd feel about shooting a man—I found out quick enough. I felt no remorse doing it, almost pleasure. In one short period of time I learned to hate as I never thought I could. I saw enough blood and torn flesh and death to last forever.... Stan Nelson and I came across a wounded kraut in a dugout and killed him. I guess hate does things to the mind...."*

I decided not to tell Lois about Johnny and Ned—not yet, anyway. I still had to wait for my own emotional wounds to heal.

TOWARD THE END of the war, Johnny's sister Evelyn wrote a note of thanks for sending the wallet to her, and for the letter of condolence. In it I lied, telling her that Johnny had gone to confession just before he died. I hid from her Johnny's last-minute expression of regret that he had not been to confession in months. In the saddest part of the letter, she wrote that the War Department telegram, "The President regrets to inform you…" had arrived on her eighteenth birthday. At first she thought it was a Happy Birthday greeting from her brother. What a terrible birthday party it must have been.

I also wrote to Ned's family. His uncle, the brother of his mother, thanked me for the letter. I heard from him again after the war when he invited me to New York for Ned's reburial in a family plot. Unfortunately, it fell during final exam week of my semester in college. I still feel guilty for not attending.

# 16:
# A Few Days' Respite

A few days later, the battle had moved past Della Torraccia, which the 86th had taken after coming around our flank, and up a deep sheltering draw. The CP was in a stone farmhouse hidden from observation by its position in a hollow about a half-mile below the ridge.

The battalion was now off the hill and on the way to Gaggio Montano. Sergeant Leisentreit sent me there to assign quarters for the company in a building he described as being the closest one near a bridge at the north end of town. The directions were adequate, and inside I found that our rucksacks were stacked in one of the rooms. I knew that Johnny had been equipped with one of the very few down sleeping bags when he went to the outpost above Gavinanna. For just a moment I wondered if swapping my blanket for the comfort of his sleeping bag would have concerned Johnny. I decided I wasn't really stealing from the dead, found his rucksack, and made the trade. HQ Company wouldn't come off the hill until morning, so I wrapped myself in the bag for a night's sleep.

When I awoke in the morning, I walked outside and found that the building had become a huge ammo dump. A hundred or more boxes of 75mm shells had been piled against its walls. Just then, a few enemy shells dropped on the street a few houses away. It didn't take long for me to realize that one shell falling near where I stood could set off the whole shebang. I wasted no time in sprinting across the bridge and to a field one hundred yards away. I stayed there until the shelling stopped, and then returned to the CP to await the company. Instinct for survival in action?

Instead of the company arriving, Bill Daniels, who I knew as a communications platoon member, drove up in Bill Blais' (the mailman's) jeep. A single truck with a few men followed.

"Where's Blais?" I asked.

"Didn't you hear? He got killed last night. He was driving through the town square when a single shell exploded. He caught a piece of shrapnel in his throat

The command post at Gaggio Montano. A German barrage threatened to blow up the stacks of artillery shells in front of the building.

(Author photo)

and died. I'm the mailman now," Daniels answered.

The mailman KIA! What a fluke accident; that was supposed to be the safest job in the company. His job was to pick up the mail at regiment and deliver it to the company CP, never to get near any danger. That shell simply had his name on it.

"Where's the company?" I asked. "They're supposed to be here by now."

"They were sent directly to Campo Tizzoro," Daniels answered. "Leisentreit sent me to guide this truck in and get you. They'll pick up the rucksacks. Hop in. I'll give you a ride there."

In less than an hour, we pulled up at the gate of an enormous villa. It was completely devoid of furniture, but the rooms were airy and clean. Leisentreit had already posted the S-2 squad in what once might have been a huge bedroom. It had an attached bathroom, but no running water. A shower unit was set up on the grounds, and we had the luxury of an almost-warm shower. Our rucksacks were delivered that afternoon, and we were able to luxuriate in clean uniforms. Our filthy ones were collected in barracks bags and delivered to a nearby laundry that Leisentreit had engaged. We came to appreciate how lucky we were to have him for a first sergeant, more with every passing day.

Tibor called Dave Williams, Stan Nelson, Pete Cantine, and me together.

This huge building in Campo Tizzoro was commandeered by the 10th Mountain Division for use as a headquarters. It had been a major ammunition factory known as Societa Metallurgica Italiana (SMI).

(Courtesy of Flint Whitlock)

To me Tibor said, "Teach these guys what we do. You'll have maybe two more days to bring them up to snuff."

Two days to show them what I learned in a year-and-a-half. Oh, boy! I gave them a quick course in map reading and the use of a compass. I showed them how to build and disguise an OP, and explained what to look and listen for. There was not enough time to teach them the intricate movements of a night patrol, but that simply meant I would be called on for that duty. Fortunately, they were all very bright and easily absorbed the essentials.

On March 2nd, our rest period at Campo Tizzoro was terminated and we were trucked to a new CP at the base of Monte Costello, which the Brazilians had taken a few days previously. The 85th was to be held there as division reserve while the other regiments resumed the attack. We could hear the sounds of battle, and at night watched the flashes of artillery shells exploding, but for the moment we were safe. Our turn would come soon enough.

We cautiously moved to Madni di Brasna and then to hills overlooking Lower Canolle, where we were to jump off. Stan and I dug in along the ridge overlooking our route of attack and watched as the battalion streamed down the hill and across the road toward their objectives.

Our troops preparing to move out from the line of departure for the attack on Monte Della Spe

(U.S. Army photo)

On March 5, 1945, the 2nd Battalion of the 85th Mountain Infantry, still reeling from the bloody battles and heavy casualties suffered in February, launched its attack. Victory did not come easily, but we suffered fewer casualties compared to our last attack.

Within two or three days, we controlled all our objectives: Lower Canolle, Monte Della Castellana, Monte Spicchione, Montesinestro, and clusters of houses at Monti and Tora. The 85th's 1st Battalion was hit much harder while taking their main objective, Monte Della Spe, and spent several days fighting vicious German counterattacks.

Our CP was moved to Lower Canolle and then to Upper Canolle where we relieved the 1st Battalion on Della Spe. Stan, Joe Carr, and Dave were sent to establish an OP near Monti. The rest of the S-2 squad and I settled into a sedentary life in the safety of a stone barn.

Captain Shepard and our battalion Sergeant Major "Dutch" DePodwin made a major contribution to our comfort. They piled a truck full of captured German helmets, gas masks, rifles, and other assorted souvenirs and headed for the port of Leghorn to see what the Navy stationed there could offer in exchange. They came

A sketch by Bob Fels of our battalion command post in the village of Upper Canolle

(Courtesy of the author)

back with a complete gasoline-powered electrical generating plant, enough wire to reach all the battalion HQ bivouacs, and dozens of bulbs and sockets. Talk about deluxe accommodations! At night I actually could sit up in my stone barn, read letters from Lois, and write a few myself.

On March 17, I wrote one to Lois—one that told about my state of mind and explained in rather grim detail how Johnny and Ned died:

*"Another lazy day went under the bridge yesterday, full of small tasks, none of which amounted to a damn. This petty existence of doing nothing is beginning to get on my nerves. Less than a month ago I was praying for a lull, and now I find myself wishing for something to do. I guess I am nuts.... Among many other reasons, I dislike the army for working me to death one minute and boring me to death the next....*

*"Johnny and Ned were both killed a month ago by artillery fire. An 88 hit two feet behind their foxhole and detonated. Johnny was nearly cut to pieces by shrapnel, and the same hunks that got Johnny got Ned. They went right through him and into Ned. It still seems hard to believe that they are dead—just a corpse and a memory. Johnny was so full of life and fun; he always had a remark to make to break the tension.... The hardest letter I ever had to help write was to Johnny's mother and dad, and Ned's too.*

*"It must have been harder on Ned's folks. He was an only child, and such a kid. He never even had time to look around and see what life was all about. He never had a girl, or went to a dance, which was amazing, considering his handsomeness. What can you say to a mother or father to compensate for the loss of a son?"*

ALMOST WITH REGRET, we were pulled out of the line on March 21. We spent one night in Passatore to the south and were then entrucked to the resort town of Montecatini and spent three days recuperating. The sad part was that whoever replaced us would claim the electrical system as their own.

Montecatini was saturated with ladies of pleasure. The story went around that removing rucksacks was the SECOND thing some of the men did. Of course, not me.

The next order of business was getting cleaned up. Hot showers and clean uniforms were a priority. Then came party time. There was a huge nightclub a few blocks from our hotel. Aside from a continuous floorshow of local talent, bottles of vino, champagne, and *grappa* (a powerful alcoholic drink made from the fermented leftovers of the winemaking process) at minuscule prices were the main attraction.

Bob Fels did this drawing of the R&R town of Montecatini. Note the "working girl" waiting for customers at far left and the GIs across the street checking out the merchandise.

(Courtesy of the author)

I hooked up with Dave Williams. We parked ourselves at a ringside table and proceeded to wash our troubles away. It took only an hour or so to polish off a few bottles of *grappa* and by then we were soused. Dave, head cupped in his hands on the table, was in much worse shape than I, and I decided to get him back to our hotel while I could still remember where it was.

At five-foot-seven, I was a wiry one-hundred-sixty pounds, hard as a rock, without an inch of flab. Dave was a six-footer and weighed close to two hundred pounds. Nevertheless, I draped him over my shoulder like a sack of wheat and made it outside to the street. Then I laid him, prostrate, on the curb and sat disconsolately next to him, wondering what to do next.

Salvation came rumbling down the cobblestone street in the form of a jeep piloted by a driver in a GI helmet. I hailed him to stop and explained that my buddy was ill, and could he please help me get him back to our hotel. Wordlessly, the man dismounted the jeep and, with difficulty, the two of us dumped Dave into the back seat. I pointed the way and soon we pulled up right in front of our hotel. The driver helped me get Dave out of the back and re-draped over my shoulder. As I turned to enter, mumbling my eternal gratitude, the shielded light on the front entrance revealed who my assistant was. He wore the silver eagle of a full colonel and the cross of a chaplain.

He never uttered a word of criticism before he drove away. Perhaps he just understood.

ALTHOUGH WE WERE on the salient of Monte Della Spe beginning March 27, early April presented two more opportunities to get away from the constant patrolling and the artillery barrages that threatened the battalion. Passover, the Jewish holiday commemorating the Exodus, fell near the end of March. Our battalion chaplain, Protestant Captain Winger, was especially considerate of those who didn't share his faith. He arranged three-day passes for Bob Fels, Harry Weinsaft, me, and several other Jews so we could go to Florence for holiday services. Dressed in wool ODs, we were trucked directly to the enormous railroad station in Florence, which had been converted into a barracks for those lucky enough to get a few days' respite. It had hundreds of cots, a sit-down mess hall (with Italians to do the KP), showers, and a dental clinic manned by dozens of dentists.

Under combat conditions, I rarely had the chance for regular brushing and my mouth felt like a garbage dump. I immediately asked for a cleaning. The clerk in charge asked if I had a toothache and when I said, "No," he announced that I wasn't eligible for dental care. Without the complaint of dental pain, they couldn't be bothered. He said it with a straight face as I observed that there were dozens of dentists standing there, yakking to each other, with nothing to do. Army rules are Army rules, stupidity notwithstanding. (As a result, when I was discharged the following January and sought private dental care, I had nearly twenty cavities filled.)

Sergeant Bob Fels, ten years my senior and a professional artist and sculptor, took me in tow. Passover services were held at an ancient and beautiful Italian synagogue just a few blocks from the railroad station. The synagogue in Florence resembled more the few Catholic churches I had visited in Italy than the temples I was familiar with in the States. Instead of a *bima* (podium) directly in front of the structure holding the sacred Torahs, the rabbi occupied an elevated platform mounted on a support pole to the congregation's right-front. He conducted much of the service from the elevated position and dismounted only to read from the Torah.

My recollection of Hebrew was pretty stale from the six years of disuse following my Bar Mitzvah, and my Italian wasn't much better, so I didn't get much from the worship ceremony.

A handful of Jewish Italians who had managed to escape the Nazi death squads occupied a few of the pews. A dozen or so GIs constituted the rest of the congregation. The Italians were too poor to provide us with a Passover feast, but the Army did back at the railroad station mess hall. I don't recall whether the meal was accompanied by traditional matzos or the standard white bread. The holiday's story recounted the tale of the Jews' first escape from tyranny. I was engaged in another.

The next day Bob took me on an enlightening tour of some Florence sites, including an art museum and Ponte Vecchio (Old Bridge). Ponte Vecchio, the oldest bridge in Florence, has shops under its stone porticos and a history going back to Roman times. That ancient bridge had miraculously escaped destruction by the fleeing Germans and was deliberately spared bombing by the advancing Americans. Spending a day immersed in art and history while we were still engaged in the destruction of human life seemed strange. Late that afternoon we were driven back to Canolle.

A few days later, early on April 6, 1945, Sergeant Leisentreit told me to get in my Class A uniform and report to the CP. A memorial service was to be held at the military cemetery near Florence, where Johnny and Ned were buried. One survivor from each 10th Mountain Division squad that had suffered a KIA was to be present; I was to represent our S-2 squad. A convoy of trucks brought us to the still-Spartan cemetery. Hundreds of markers, each bearing a dog tag of the deceased, were lined up in the little valley. Here, rank did not matter. Privates and officers were buried next to each other. Grass had not yet grown over many of the graves. We lined up at attention and saluted as the sound of "Taps" echoed from the valley walls. Afterward, we broke rank, and I found Johnny and Ned's graves and stifled farewell tears. We left immediately thereafter for the long, quiet ride back to the front.

The ornate Jewish synagogue in Florence

(Courtesy of the author)

A vintage postcard showing the Ponte Vecchio over the Arno River in Florence

(Courtesy Flint Whitlock)

My parents wept for joy when I sent them this picture of me taken by a street photographer in Florence (paid for with a pack of American cigarettes, the unofficial official currency) because it proved to them that I was alive and well.

(Author photo)

# 17: Prelude to the End

Headquarters Company was still scattered throughout the cluster of ancient, shell-pocketed stone buildings at Upper Canolle. The village huddled against the southern shoulder of Monte Della Spe, which the 1st Battalion had taken a few weeks before, but only after suffering massive casualties. Our 2nd Battalion rifle companies, reinforced with mortar and machine-gun squads from the weapons company, had relieved them and were now solidly entrenched in deep, zigzag scars amidst shrapnel-shattered tree stumps on the peak's terrain.

The foxholes were deep enough to stand in, with angled tunnels at the bottom. They provided nearly complete protection against artillery airbursts and a place to stretch out for a decent night's sleep. Used ammo and ration boxes and sections of fallen trees provided reinforcement for the walls, but there was always the possibility of a cave-in from a near miss. Deep trenches connected sandbagged bunkers that became command posts for the squads and platoons and companies. Thus shielded from the storm of shrapnel and long-distance machine-gun fire, remnants of depleted squads guarded the hard-won gains.

Lieutenant Colonel S. made a rare foray to the front and inspected the defensive positions. Despite the elaborate entrenchments, reminiscent of World War I, the only arrangement for a safe toilet disposal of feces was "do it on a shovel and toss it out." S. accidentally stepped in such a site and upon returning to Canolle issued an order that read, "Indiscriminate defecation on the hillside will cease immediately." Not a word of praise for our courage. Not a word of encouragement in recognition of our accomplishments. That order did nothing to alleviate the battalion's disdain for him.

SIGNS OF AN impending attack were everywhere. Mountainous stacks of shells, rations, and ammo boxes filled the gullies and ravines a mile or so behind our positions. Each battalion had, in rotation, spent a few riotous days in the bars and whorehouses of Montecatini. Now, freshly showered, clad in newly laundered uniforms, we were sent on frequent patrols with emphasis on taking prisoners and pinpointing German positions. We mapped their minefields, bunkers, and gun emplacements. Another sign was the road-improving activity conducted by our engineers with their little mountain bulldozers. They tried to make highways out of nearly impassible mule trails. Unarmed Italian Alpini mountain troops, now our co-belligerents, bivouacked with their mule trains at regimental supply dumps, ready to ferry supplies to us as we advanced. There was no question about it. We *would* advance.

One day, Shep's familiar, white-granite face appeared above the sandbagged sill of the hut window, where I was bedded down in a hay-filled mattress that was the GI version of a Beautyrest. "Daneman, do you want to take a walk?" he asked, disturbing my afternoon nap. Shep's restlessness was absolute proof that the jump-off was near.

A few minutes later we took off for the mountain peak at the gentle pace the steepness required. My canteen was full, an extra bandoleer of ammo for my M-1 was draped across my shoulder, grenades and K-rations bulged in my mountain-jacket pockets. In less than an hour we reached the maze of trenches and foxholes at the top. A few lookouts manned the outposts while other GIs burrowed in their nests. They diligently, almost lovingly, cleaned and oiled their weapons. A few sat with bayonet-sharpened pencil stubs scratching out what might be their last V-mail home. We checked the password with the outpost guards and told them we were going out on a reconnaissance. They should keep their itchy fingers off their triggers until they were sure it was Germans and not us coming back on the trail.

With a round in the chamber and safety off, I let my rifle point the way as I led, tentatively, down a sketchy trail running diagonally across the face of the forward slope at Monte Della Spe. In a few yards, the trail widened into a deeply embanked cart track. With painstaking caution, on the lookout for mines, tripwires, booby traps, snipers, or any sign of an ambush, we crept ahead. Here and there were mortar pits dug by the Germans during their counterattacks. Spent machine-gun cartridges littered the ground, and nearby lay a German helmet flanked by a bullet-riddled American one. An unfired *Panzerfaust*, a German antitank rocket similar to the American bazooka, leaned against the embankment. In deep shade, a stone hut appeared through the foliage below us.

"Cover me!" Shep commanded quietly. He slipped through the trees bordering the trail toward the hut. I huddled against the embankment, rifle aimed at the building's only window. There appeared to be no movement inside. In a few moments I saw Shep waving me forward.

"Empty," he whispered, and motioned me to take the lead again.

A few minutes later we were creeping through a ditch at the edge of the hard-surfaced road running along the base of the mountain. I kept watch to our flanks while Shep peered through his binoculars at the buildings dotting the meadow across the road. The maps we carried called the place Pra del Bianco. The lengthening shadows hid the draws and ravines on the hills beyond, through which Shep was seeking routes of advance to use in the forthcoming attack. Soon, he signaled me to work my way back to the hidden cart track. We paused there to regroup.

"Let's get over toward the west side of the peak," Shep ordered. He took the lead and climbed the lower edge of the embankment, leaving us exposed to the Germans through a thin line of trees. He took off running in a zigzag trot on a route paralleling our battalion's positions on the peak above. I followed in his tracks, twenty yards behind, expecting to hear the crash of mortars, the crack of bullets, or the eruption of a *Schu* mine. But none came. On the western ridge, overlooking the shelled ruins of Castel d'Aiano, we warily worked our way up a draw to our own positions. We answered a sentry's muffled challenge with the password, and re-entered our lines.

We climbed into a heavily sandbagged machine-gun position and exited into a path of winding trenches that were shored up with a network of branches from fallen trees. A circuitous one hundred feet brought us to a well-dug-in company command post. Shep bantered with the company commander for a few minutes, who then asked us to check out some abandoned houses in a draw running down off his left flank. The group of houses was called Famaticca. Although Famaticca had long since been deserted by the owners, the outposts had heard noises from that direction during the night.

That was an invitation Shep couldn't refuse. Soon we were creeping down a steep gully. The huts, near the base of Della Spe, were half-hidden in deep underbrush near the ravine's bottom. For what seemed like hours, we listened. While I kept watch for a German patrol, Shep inspected every door and window with his binoculars. Only half-convinced that they were unoccupied, we approached the buildings from the gully's steep banks, uphill, on their blind side. Again we watched and listened. No noise or movement. At last convinced that we were alone, we worked our way around to the little clearing they faced, arranged like wagons drawn into a circle. We felt around the doors for tripwires. None. They were not booby trapped as far as we could tell.

The rooms looked empty, but we didn't tempt fate by entering. Leaving "downtown Famaticca," I led the way down a few more yards to Della Spe's base. From there, a wide, tree-covered ledge ran back to our lines, and to the outposts guarding Canolle. Again I led, watching for the telltale prongs of buried mines and gingerly feeling for tripwires in the trees. Darkness began to fall. Suddenly, a few yards ahead,

A dead German lies in the rubble of a destroyed building.

(Author photo)

two prone figures appeared. I swung my rifle down to shoot, finger tight on the trigger. Another step revealed that they were not moving. They lay on their backs, eyes staring vacantly at the sky. Their gray uniforms confirmed their identity: two dead Germans.

Now at my side, Shep warned, "Careful, they might be booby-trapped." A gentle prod with my rifle could not move a grotesquely angled leg—rigor mortis had frozen the pose. They had been dead more than a few hours but the stench of death had not yet begun. I carefully removed the *Wehrmacht* pay books protruding from their gray tunic pockets. The books would reveal their units, and that would interest regimental and division intelligence.

"Okay, let's just leave them and report where they are," I suggested. "Someone can come back tomorrow with some rope and drag them a bit to make sure they are clean."

Another cautious two hundred yards through the heavy brush brought a challenge from our concealed outpost, and an exchanged password. We headed for the CP, where Shep went in to make his sketches and map out what we had seen. Armed with the German pay books, I sought out Tibor who would forward them up the line. Then I returned to the comfort of my hay-filled mattress. The stress of the past few hours settled in my gut. When I stopped shivering, I sat down to a dinner of cold K-ration: Chopped ham, a cement-hard and bitter chocolate bar, and a Fleetwood cigarette. Then I crawled into my sleeping bag and resumed my restless sleep.

# 18:
# Pra del Bianco, the Valley of Death

The jump-off was close enough to smell. Shep pulled me out of the S-2 squad again and designated me as battalion guide, a fictitious slot in the Table of Organization. I could read a map and had some patrol experience as well as a good sense of direction that could lead me back to a dime after a ten-mile hike in the dark. My first mission alone would send me back to Madna di Brasa, the little village housing the regimental replacement pool. I was to bring back, as fresh fodder, a hundred or so men to fill the gaps in the decimated battalion's roster.

I took what looked like the easy way there, fully exposed on the road through Castel d'Aiano. It was too far a shot for a German sniper, and they couldn't afford to waste artillery or mortars on a single GI.

The destroyed town of Castel d'Aiano

(U.S. Army photo)

Castel d'Aiano as it appears today.

(Courtesy of the author)

The town was an utter ruin; few buildings weren't heavily damaged or destroyed. Broken glass, half-demolished furniture, and broken masonry littered the cobblestone streets and alleys. A jeep, all four tires flattened by shrapnel, sat in the middle of the town square amid the rubble. An occasional GI poked a helmeted head over a foxhole's parapet, or stood in a dugout's door, and waved a silent greeting as I ambled by. An easy hour's walk brought me to the regiment's replacement pool.

It was astonishingly well organized. I announced to an officer that I was there to get the 2nd Battalion replacements. Ten minutes later I was leading a column of scared replacements—privates, non-coms, and shavetails—toward their first encounter with terror. Only days before they had been administrative clerks at some airbase or supply depot, or a cipher at a Repo-Depo. The shortage of riflemen and the injustice of war had brought them here.

I led them cross-country, directly toward Canolle, on rolling meadows flanked by protective hills, finding defilade where I could to avoid enemy observation. Now our numbers made us an inviting artillery target, and the use of even shallow gullies kept us hidden from their OPs. With five yards between each man, the line stretched over a quarter mile. I sent an officer to the tail end to prod stragglers along. When we reached a point just under the crest of a ridge overlooking a deep canyon, beyond which Canolle huddled, I broke the column into four groups. By the authority of my two stripes and my status as a combat veteran, I put an officer in charge of each group. I pointed to a rendezvous spot across the gorge and—from separated points on the ridge—sent them running at full speed down its sides.

The men arrived at the rendezvous within minutes of each other, breathless and sweating, but without drawing a single round of artillery or mortar fire. Hidden from observation by the shoulder of Della Spe, we continued the march to Canolle and the battalion CP. Soon they were divided into herds, like cattle, and dispatched to the rifle and weapons platoons. Wide-eyed, dry-mouthed, in petrified silence, they followed their company guides up the winding trails to the peaks to fill the foxholes still stained by the blood of the men they were to replace.

A DAY OR TWO later Shep came at dusk with his usual question, "Daneman, do you want to take a walk?"

The attack was now set for mid-April, just a few days away. Shep had grumbled that the last recon we made was inadequate. The information about the terrain was too sketchy, and he was intent on getting another look, because he had to send the battalion headquarters personnel forward during the height of the coming battle, and he didn't want to do it blind. My job would be to guide them, and he wanted me to have a second look, too.

A large recon patrol could not penetrate without being detected as deeply into German positions as we needed to go. Shep thought just the two of us would have a better chance, especially under the bright artificial moonlight that the distant spotlights would bring.

By 2200 hours (10:00 p.m.), we had passed through our alerted outposts and proceeded stealthily down the trail on the face of Della Spe and through the defiladed cart track to the bottom of the peak. We crossed the road where heavy shadows cast by the trees gave us some protection from observation. We crouched in a clump of bushes, well forward of our lines at the eastern edge of Hill 860. We stumbled on a patrol from the 87th Regiment and were lucky they mistook us as part of their group and didn't start shooting in the confusion. Intent on their own mission, they started off to the east. We slipped through the thickening timber to explore Hill 822 to the west.

Methodically, silently, we tiptoed up the slope, pausing every few steps to listen and look. We emerged from a draw onto a sheltered, grassy knoll—a perfect place for the CP. The hills to its north would shield it from German observation once we took those positions. When Shep felt satisfied about finding a suitable place, we slipped quietly downhill toward our own positions nearly a thousand yards to the south, seeking a viable route home.

I took the lead, gingerly groping through the undergrowth, eyes darting everywhere, seeking deadly traps. Suddenly, I felt a smooth wire brush my hand. Tripwire? I hit the dirt, expecting the blast of a booby trap. None came—no sound but my labored breath. Shep, ten feet behind me, had ducked when I did. Now he crept to my side and asked a whispered, "What's up?"

"Smooth wire," I whispered in return.

"Back marker of their minefield," Shep cursed. It was the universal technique of warning one's own troops that a minefield lay ahead.

Standing, I looped my fingers around the wire and let it slip through my hand as I eased back toward the eastern end of the hill, seeking to locate the safe route through which we had come. Could we repeat the miracle that had brought us, unscathed, through a German minefield in the dark?

We had gone perhaps fifty yards when two standing figures suddenly materialized in the shadows.

"Shep! Krauts!" I hissed, and swung my rifle toward them, prepared to shoot. Shep brought his carbine to bear. As I began to press the trigger, "*Kamerad*" came the hoarse cry from one of the figures. They stumbled toward us, trembling, faces terror-filled, hands high over their heads. They had discarded their rifles and a quick pat-down revealed no hidden arms or grenades. Luckily for us, they were determined to surrender. They could easily have blasted us, but battle-worn, disillusioned, and broken spirited, they wanted only to survive these last days of war. I pointed to the long meadow now separating us from the foot of Monte Della Spe.

"*Minen*?" I whispered in a quizzical tone.

"*Ja, ja, ja*," came the guttural response. I jabbed a finger into one German's chest and growled, "You first." I pointed across the field.

"*Ja*," he answered. The Germans moved a few yards downhill through a gap in the wire, and then trod on a carefully measured zigzag course through the grass.

The second Kraut silently pointed after his comrade, then to himself. I nodded and he followed. I walked behind them and Shep brought up the rear. In silence, we reached the shelter of the cart road at the foot of Della Spe as the first streaks of dawn stained the sky above Rocco Roffeno to the east.

Now we had our first good look at our prisoners. The talkative one was an "old man," perhaps thirty-five, with a deeply lined face, unshaven for maybe a week. His uniform was caked with mud and he shivered with fright. He knew we would no longer need him to bring us through the minefield and he probably wondered if we would kill him.

The other prisoner was a boy, not over fifteen or sixteen, pale and palsied with fear. He shook with dread as I reached into my pocket, and then he sighed and wept with relief when I pulled out a crushed pack of cigarettes. I offered one to each and lit one for myself. I watched as their shaking hands lit my Zippo, and as they drew deeply on their cigarettes. Then they smiled. They had won a deadly gamble. They had survived.

Shep led the procession up the hill to our positions. At the first challenge, Shep answered with the password and added, "Patrol coming in with prisoners." Otherwise, the two figures in German gray might have made the lookouts nervous and brought on a rain of fire and grenades. We prodded the prisoners along, past curious clumps of staring GIs. An hour later, after Tibor verified their units by examining their pay books, we turned the POWs over to a regimental collection point. Shep presented me with the "receipt" as a souvenir. I stuck it in my pocket and somehow lost it later.

We returned to Canolle, and Shep went into the Battalion CP while I prepared my hay-filled mattress for some shut-eye in the stone hut. Tibor rousted me out in a few minutes, telling me to report to S-2 Lieutenant James.

"What did I do now?" I asked myself. "Did I fuck something up?"

I was met by James, who led me a few yards away from the CP.

"Daneman," he said, "I just want to tell you that I was wrong. I never felt fully comfortable having a city boy like you in the squad, but I've changed my mind. I heard what you did on Belvedere and what you did tonight. You're a pretty damn good scout."

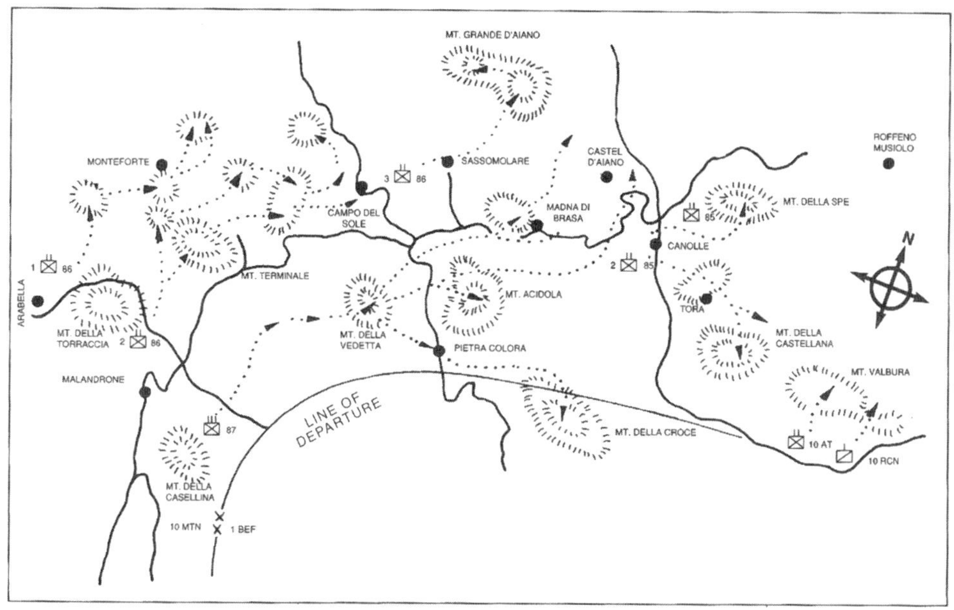


Map of combat actions in the Mt. Della Spe area

My face turned red. I murmured an embarrassed, “Thanks.” I didn’t know what else to say. That night Shep wrote me up for a Bronze Star, but only for Belvedere. Maybe he was saving tonight for another.

## 19:
## The Final Push

The attack was launched a few days later. It was a "major offensive" called Operation Craftsman, with both the U.S. Fifth Army, on the western half of Italy, and the British Eighth Army, on the eastern half, plus all Allied tactical aircraft and some 50,000 Italian partisans taking part. The objective was to throw everything the Allies had against the Germans and finally break out of the mountains and into the Po Valley.

I had a box seat in the battalion observation post, just forward of the crest of Della Spe. We'd had a false alarm the day before, a postponement because of bad weather. Rumors also attributed the delay to President Roosevelt's death. Most of us believed that, but the postponement was really weather that prevented tactical air support.

On the big day—April 14, 1945—Air Corps P-47s laid a torrent of steel and fire on the ridges where Shep and I had prowled a few nights before. Then our division artillery, backed by Corps' 155mm Long Toms manned by gutsy Tommies, threw a crushing barrage. Thousands of rounds of shells crashed into German positions, and a pallor of smoke slid down the hillsides and filled the valley.

"Nothing could survive that cauldron of hell-fire," I thought. But then I remembered how the well-entrenched Germans survived a similar pasting on Della Torraccia just a few weeks before. I knew the SOBs would still be there to send their own deluge of steel into our troops. And the mines, sown everywhere, would take their own victims.

At 0900 hours, our heavy machine guns and 81mm mortars opened up at long range with a creeping barrage. They laid down their patterns of fire close in front of our line of departure, then gradually moving, increased their range as our troops began to move forward. The riflemen began their descent down the face of Della Spe to the road below. Now came the German return fire—mortars, 88s, and the rapid staccato of their machine guns. In a ravine to my right, a mortar barrage dropped on one of our platoons, mortally wounding a second lieutenant I had brought in as a replacement only days before. He died without firing a shot, or even crossing the line of departure. His name was Callahan, and a highway tunnel in Boston has been dedicated to his memory.

Another platoon filed silently past, then trotted over the embankment and across a potato patch. A German barrage sent them scurrying back, dragging their wounded. One of them crawled into my OP, his back bleeding from the gaping entry wound of a shrapnel shard. It had just missed hitting his spine. I took his first-aid kit, poured sulfa into the wound, and tied a bandage in place. He knew he was lucky. Had we heard air sucking through the wound, it would have meant a lung wound, from which he would have bled to death. He became one of the walking wounded and headed back to the aid station at Canolle. The platoon's medic worked on a more seriously wounded man who would obviously require evacuation on a stretcher.

The platoon leader came hobbling back, cheerfully announcing that he had taken a sliver of shrapnel in his calf, the "million-dollar wound" which would get him safely out of combat. Although limping, and obviously in pain, he joined the walking wounded headed for the aid station. He was a gutsy second lieutenant and rejoined his platoon as soon as he was patched up.

The platoon sergeant, now in charge, reorganized his men to re-enter the attack. I suggested to him that they go further down the cart track, which offered some defilade. This time they made their dash down the hill and into the fray without drawing fire.

The noise of the battle raged all day with most of the action screened from the OP by smoke. I could surmise that we were advancing by the gradual diminishing volume of rifle fire. Just before dusk, Shep came to me, not with an offer to take a walk, but leading the HQ advance platoon. A gap had opened between G and E Companies, through which the Krauts were infiltrating snipers to our rear. The platoon was to occupy the western flank of Hill 822, seal the gap, and open the forward CP so the companies could resume the advance. Shep and I were to position them.

By now, paths had been cleared through the minefields in the meadow where the Germans had led Shep and me a few nights before. Illuminated by the reflected artificial moonlight of the huge searchlights on the hills behind us, the twisted safe paths were outlined by white tape stretched between stakes. The path ended just below the foot of the gully where I had hit the smooth wire. Shep, at the head of the line, started up the draw.

I recognized the terrain. "Shep, this is where the mines are."

"Naw, they were in the next draw over," he replied.

"Shep, they were here!"

Eyes narrowing, he said, "Daneman, get back to the end of the line and make sure there are no stragglers."

"Shep...," I started to insist, but he had already resumed walking up the draw with the platoon following. I turned away, took a few downhill steps, and was knocked down by a blast from behind. Then another. Stunned, dazed by the concussion, I sat at the edge of the field while a medic rushed up the draw toward the screams of pain. The platoon's radio man had stepped on a mine. Shep turned to help him and triggered a *Schu* mine, which blew up in his crotch and exploded. Lieutenant James, who had been about to enter the draw, saw what happened and came down to comfort me.

I had been right. This *was* the mined draw, not yet swept clean.

Why hadn't I tried harder to convince him that I was right about that minefield? Why hadn't I yelled at him, "YOU'RE WRONG, YOU DUMB SONOFABITCH. I KNOW IT!"

I still ask myself that question, even in my sleep. Shep died in a moment or two. James told me Shep's last words were, "What have I done now?"

Shep's tragic death left me shattered. I had experienced the loss of my two closest friends, Johnny and Ned, and now my mentor was gone. I felt anchorless and alone. A pervasive depression filled my soul. For a long time I just sat on the edge of the woods until, eventually, Jessie came back. He put his arm around my shoulder and, with a gentleness I had never previously heard in his voice, said, "You don't want to see him. What's left isn't pretty. Why don't you just go back to the CP?"

I crossed the meadow at Pra del Bianco, keeping well within the tape-marked cleared passages. Slowly I climbed along the cart track toward the peak of Della Spe. The *karumph* of exploding shells echoed from beyond the crest. When I approached the trench line at the top, Sergeant Savage looked up at me from the bottom of a trench and announced, "I'm hit. I caught a piece in my leg." He had already applied his first-aid patch and refused my offer to lend him a hand.

"Naw, this here's a million-dollar wound. Just a little hole in my calf. I'm going back to the aid station. They were getting ready to move the CP when I left."

"Where to?"

"Bottom of the hill you just came up."

So I headed back down to await the rest of HQ, not knowing where the S-2 squad was. There was no sign of anyone when I reached the valley floor. Since it was already getting dark, I headed for the ruins of a stone house at Serra Sarzana at the foot of Hill 860 to see if I could find a safe spot, finish a can of C-rations, and bed down. The house was in bad shape, but a stairway ran up the one standing wall and an open door hinted at a still-remaining room nestled against a hillside. I warily climbed the steps, ready for anything, and found what must have been a German outpost: bed, blankets, and all. I hastily downed a can of franks and beans, munched a few crackers, took a long swig from my canteen, and shook the blankets free of vermin. In a few minutes I was deep in an exhausted sleep.

Early in the morning, the house started to tremble under the reverberations of heavy artillery. I rolled out of bed, ready to head for any handy hole. A glimpse around the edge of a remaining wall revealed the source of the noise. A battery of British Long Toms, their equivalent to our 155mm heavy artillery, had moved into the edge of Pra del Bianco during the night, set up while I slept, and greeted the dawn with a barrage of direct fire against some German positions on the hills above.

Relieved, I made it down the stairs and toward the houses clustered around the meadow, looking for some sign of the CP. A few yards from the ruin, I was astonished to find the parts of a disassembled German Walther P-38 pistol. Somehow I found the right sequence of assembly, put it together, pumped a shell into the chamber, and shot a round into the ground. Miracle of miracles, I had the souvenir of a lifetime, and a personal legal sidearm.

As I walked along the cleared narrow path, two men unreeling telephone wire from a large drum hailed me to ask where they could find the 2nd Battalion commanding officer.

"He's probably up this hill," I said. "I'm looking for him, too."

"Show us where," they urged. "We've got to get this line from regiment to him."

I turned up the hill, following the taped path. As we climbed up the slope, an artillery barrage began to fall one hundred yards or so ahead of us. I turned toward the two men but saw only a glimpse of their backs as they ran back toward the base of the hill and disappeared in the distance. The reel of wire lay abandoned on the hillside just below me. It dawned on me that a message from regiment to the battalion CO was probably important, so I turned the reel on edge and began the Herculean task of rolling it uphill. At the crest I came across several men in foxholes.

"Anyone seen Lieutenant Colonel S.?" I asked.

"Over there," one answered, pointing to a trench to my right.

Several officers stood in it, scanning the next hill with binoculars. I rolled the reel over and dropped it into the trench.

"Sir," I said to S., "regiment is trying to reach you, but the men bringing up the wire didn't leave a phone."

One of the officers, who I recognized as our S-3 operations officer, Captain McIntyre, disconnected a phone from another wire and slipped its wires into connectors on the reel. In a moment, S. was carrying on a muffled conversation as I stood only a few feet from him. Shortly afterward, he announced to those within hearing, "I've just been relieved."

I could hardly contain myself or suppress a smile of satisfaction as I climbed out of the back of the trench and headed back down the hill. It was Lieutenant Colonel S.'s ineptitude that had allowed the battalion's attack to stall on the chestnut-covered ridge beyond Belvedere—where Johnny and Ned died. Lieutenant Colonel S. had carried the mantle of prissiness all the way from Camp Hale. Most of the troops felt nothing but disgust for him. A month earlier, I had written Lois a letter that pretty much summed up my feelings toward S.: *"He still puts out orders that a moron would have better sense to, and worse still, is the same inconsiderate, holier-than-thou, chicken-minded, self-centered louse that he was. If you weren't a lady, I'd use a better description than that."*

I SILENTLY GLOATED as I followed the taped path back across the meadow toward Pra del Bianco, wondering where to go next. A truck careened past me, charging across the taped path to the foot of the gully where Shep had died, and slid to a stop. Before I could yell to him, one of the occupants jumped off the truck, triggering a *Schu* mine. He was in a crouch following the jump, and the savagery of the

This farmhouse, photographed during a return trip to Italy in the 1970s, was the aid station to which I carried the mortally wounded Hugh Craven.

(Author photo)

blast barely nicked his foot before passing over his head. But another man, Hugh Craven, sitting next to the open tailgate, took the full blast in his stomach. He slumped sideways and fell unconscious to the ground. Everyone started yelling for a medic. When none responded, I ran back to the truck, picked up Craven, and carried him, like an infant, in my arms more than four hundred yards to an aid station. I'll never know where I got that kind of strength, since Craven outweighed me by twenty-five pounds.

When I got inside, I laid him on an empty litter. I grabbed a medic by the arm and dragged him over. "He's hit. Do *something*!"

The medic leaned over, looked at the wound through which shreds of intestines were pushing, at the face with eyes rolled up out of sight, and at the cold pallor of impending death. Glancing my way, he announced, "He ain't going to make it. I got to fix up one who will," and turned away to tend to another man.

Many years later, I learned the proper word for that situation is "triage": Do for the wounded what will have a life-saving effect. Don't waste time and effort on the unsalvageable. I was stunned that Craven would be allowed to die, but the medic was right. There were other wounded men he could save.

Three GIs escort a group of fourteen German prisoners (one of whom is being carried on a litter by four of his comrades) to the rear area in the Po Valley.

(Author photo)

What's left of a German convoy along the Po River—after Allied air power got finished with it

(U.S. Army photo)

When I got back to the site where the truck was parked, I saw someone backing it out along the entry tire marks to avoid other mines. I realized that this was the mess truck—those aboard had all been cooks. The kitchen crew had already received orders to proceed to a steep valley a few miles to the northeast where battalion headquarters was regrouping. When the truck reached the main road, I climbed aboard and took the seat where Craven had sustained his fatal wounds. Life goes on.

## 20:
## On to and across the Po River

It was dark when the mess truck pulled into a valley with sharply pitched sides. I watched while the shaken remnants of our cook staff set up a kitchen under Mess Sergeant LePore's urgent prompting. In the States, he had been considered a ruthless tyrant, but here, in a combat zone, his true colors emerged. He would move heaven and earth to get his company fed with their first hot meal in days. It would also be our last one for a couple of weeks.

In a few minutes I could see that a tent had been set up to house the CP, and those digging in had familiar faces. HQ Company was to be reunited! By artificial moonlight I could see that the canyon walls were so steep it would be difficult to find a level place to sleep, so I scraped out a shallow but level trench. There were no fir trees there whose branches would have made a comfortable mattress, but I was too tired to care.

I had just finished making my bed when Stan and Tibor came to me with a proposition. As a member of the S-2 squad, Stan was entitled to a sleeping bag—the very one I had lifted from Johnny's rucksack at Gaggio Montano. He had filched a GI quilt from who-knows-where and had it sewn into a makeshift sleeping bag. He was willing to trade it for the real sleeping bag. Tibor nodded to seal the deal. Well, he was entitled to it, so I didn't make a fuss, and his contraption would be just as warm and just as light. I obviously lived in a world of compromise, and I kept my friendship with Stan.

The battalion headquarters stragglers began to filter in. Sergeant Leisentreit told me to pick an area for each platoon and have them set up a perimeter defense. That done, I gulped down some chow and hot coffee and managed a few hours' sleep. We were aroused before dawn and gathered up our rucksacks that had been brought up during the night. It would be good to have a badly needed change of socks and underwear.

The next few days were a confusion of intermittent marching marked by the usual bunching up as long columns of troops competed for the few narrow roads.

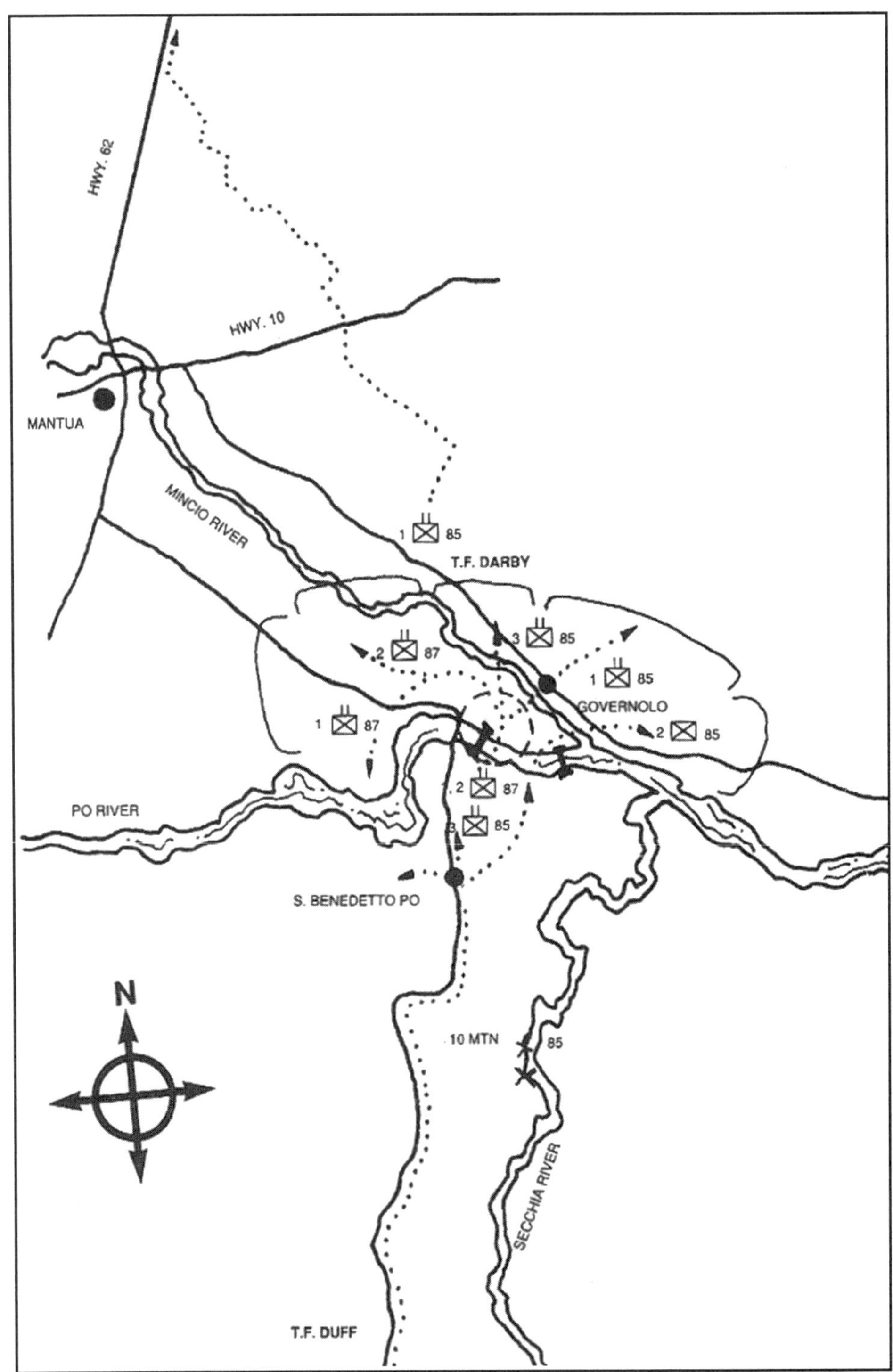


Route of the 10th from the Apennines into the Po Valley (From *Soldiers on Skis*)

Occasionally I was sent with a patrol on a reconnaissance to check out a meandering side road or check on a cluster of houses on a nearby knoll. Italian citizens brought us reports of the whereabouts of stray German troops, who had to be rousted out and taken prisoner. An occasional stray artillery or mortar shell sometimes fell near us as we marched, but the battalion moved gradually, inexorably, north.

The stress of the past weeks began to take its toll. When shells hit the ground more than a hundred yards away, much too far to be threatening, I found myself hitting the ground. Was I approaching crack-up time? I had to steel myself to march on.

We wended our way through hills that became less and less intimidating as we approached the Po Valley. Still, we kept to military discipline, maintaining at least five yards between men, and twenty or more yards between columns. The weather now clearly spoke of spring and forthcoming summer. Our layers of clothing melted into our rucksacks, and most of us were down to wearing a single set of underwear under our ODs; the long-johns were no longer needed. We kept our mountain jackets on to satisfy the need for voluminous pockets, into which we stuffed several days' rations.

Suddenly, as we marched one morning, the hills virtually disappeared, and the terrain became gently rolling. We crossed what we knew was the main highway marking the edge of the Po Valley. We had reached the Promised Land, and it was absolutely awe-inspiring. One hundred miles to the north, toward the Austrian border, we thought we could see the faint images of towering peaks of the Alps. Another damn set of mountains to fight in.

THE FIRST NIGHT in the Po Valley found me footsore and weary after a long day's march. We stopped in a small cluster of houses and, too tired to really dig in, I found the dubious shelter of a farm wagon parked in the yard. In the morning, Harry Leisentreit came to me, concerned about the lack of firepower in our crew of HQ personnel. If we had to engage in any kind of a firefight, Harry fretted, it wouldn't take much to have us severely outgunned. In the confusion of the rapid advance, HQ sometimes led the march.

"I'm going to carry your rucksack and rifle in my jeep," Harry said. "I want you to take the .30-caliber machine gun with the bipod, mount it on a packboard, and be the company's main defense."

I did a quick mental calculation: The filled rucksack weighed about forty pounds. My M-1 weighed about eight pounds. Add to that my two bandoliers of ammo, and I was carrying fifty-five pounds or so. The machine gun weighed only about forty pounds. Fair enough. I got Pete Cantine and one other man similar deals if they would carry only their rifles and the ammo boxes. Thus unburdened, we set off again.

The evolving strategy had some troops marching aggressively north, some troops resting, and a third group on trucks catching up to, and relieving, those who were marching. One day we marched a foot-blistering twenty-three miles; the hard training at Camp Swift paid off. When it was our turn aboard the trucks, we approached a crucial bridge at Bomporto, and there was our commanding general, General Hays, standing at its entrance, directing traffic. His fully exposed presence there confirmed our appreciation of his courage.

As we marched over the zigzag network of dusty roads, the Italians lined up along the way and offered us bottles of vino and loaves of freshly baked bread. Unlike our previous experiences in Naples and the Apennines, the Po Valley was the breadbasket of Italy, and there didn't seem to be a food shortage.

For a time, we took to wide, grass-covered fields and marched cross-country by azimuth when the road network became too indirect, or when canals interrupted our most direct line of advance. As we passed a mile or so to the east of the village of Carpi,* I heard the sound of sporadic gunfire. Harry sent me and a couple of others in his jeep to check it out, because if there were organized German units on our flank or rear, they could be a menace. We shortly ascertained that E Company had been given the same mission and returned to the marching HQ Company without mishap.

OUR NEW COMPANY commander, Captain Russ Gullixson, wasn't really familiar with our ad hoc Table of Organization and the invented position of battalion guide. He asked Harry for someone to help him assign quarters as we prepared to bivouac at an Italian farm that night. Harry told him that had been my job under Captain Shepard, and I was reassigned to that position. I gave up the machine gun and resumed my battalion guide functions. I posted the HQ personnel in a defensive circle around the farm with instructions that everyone pair off with another man and alternate standing guard. I reserved a spot in the farm's hayloft for me and got a good night's sleep.

---

* Many years later I learned that the great opera singer, Luciano Pavarotti, then a young teen, had been sent to the safety of Carpi from his home in nearby Modena and was part of the welcoming horde. When he performed in my hometown of Dallas, Lois and I, as active opera supporters, were invited to a post-opera dinner and met him there. As soon as I related the story to him, he stopped eating, dropped his knife and fork, stood up, and called me his liberator while giving me the bear hug of my life. I treasure the photo taken as he wrapped his arms around me.

After giving me a big bear hug, the famed operatic tenor Luciano Pavarotti signs his autograph for Lois and me at a benefit in Dallas. He was grateful for our unit liberating the village of Carpi, where he had taken refuge as a boy.

(Author photo)

I spent the next day with Gullixson and Sergeant Major Dutch Depodwin in the company commander's jeep. We rode in style ahead of the marching company, which this time was following one of the line companies for protection. All I had to do now was set up a suitable defensive position each night. It sure beat walking, but my riding days ended abruptly when I had to relinquish my jeep seat to another officer or two. Marching with the rest of the company meant I arrived at the same

A GI inspects a large, knocked-out piece of German armor left behind by the retreating foe.

(Author photo)

moment they did. Thereafter, I had to ad lib the defensive positions, at night, usually without really having a chance to check things out.

I decided, perhaps unfairly, that I didn't have the same kind of blind attachment to Gullixson that I'd had for Shep. My resentment grew, and I asked Tibor if he could arrange to get me back in the S-2 squad. He was now operating with three untrained scouts and welcomed the chance to get an "old hand" back. He went to Leisentreit, who understood completely. (I don't think he had any kind of feeling for Gullixson, either.) I again became the assistant squad leader of the S-2 squad.

We arrived at the Po River in daylight and dug in at a farm a kilometer or so south of the river. We heard distant artillery fire as the 87th crossed to our west, and we took desultory shelling with "very light" casualties. (I put that in quotes because I know of only one man in our battalion who was hit while we awaited our crossing orders.) I watched the scene, numb with horror and shock, as an old Italian civilian man wept at the sight of medics trying to alleviate the suffering of the wounded GI. He had most of one leg destroyed by shrapnel. The leg was laid open to the bone from groin to ankle, and it was obvious that if he lived, he would lose the leg. The medic already had pumped a vial of morphine into the trembling body, but it did little to alleviate the terrible pain.

Amphibious DUKWs ("Ducks") prepare to cross the wide Po River with troops and supplies prior to a temporary bridge being built by Army engineers.

(Author photo)

"Mama! Mama!" came the agonized cry from the wounded man. "Mama! Mama! It hurts!"

I turned away in frustration and anger as the medic poured sulfa into the gaping wound and prepared a second vial of morphine. The old man continued to weep and I tried to comfort him with an arm over his shoulder. He had ridden to the scene on his decrepit bicycle. I helped him mount it and sent him on his way. So much for "very light" casualties.

We were hidden from the river by high dikes. Stan and I did a recon of the opposite side with field glasses while stretched out atop the dike. There appeared to be unmanned fortifications on the other side, but we never could be sure. Later that night, as our line companies crossed the river, we were strafed by an unidentified aircraft. To this day, I feel the airplane was one of ours, the pilot not realizing we had advanced so far.

Just before dusk it was HQ Company's turn to cross the Po, which looked to be about a thousand yards wide. At this point Harry was to leave his jeep, so I traded the machine gun for my M-1 and left my rucksack to be reclaimed later. Huddling behind the dike, an engineer explained what we were supposed to do. Each of us was handed a paddle. We were to run over the top of the embankment to the river's edge, toss our rifles into a waiting flat-bottomed boat, grab the gunwale, carry the boat into the river until it floated, jump in, and paddle like crazy until we reached the other side. When we hit the opposite bank, we were to drop our paddles in the boat, grab our rifles, and do whatever the guide on the opposite bank instructed.

Two engineers accompanied us. It was their job to steer and then get the boat back to the south bank for another run. Simple. Surprisingly, the whole process went without a hitch. We did exactly as we were told. Silently we scrambled up the bank and down to the water's edge where a boat awaited us. We tumbled into the boat and frantically paddled for the other side, expecting the scream of a shell, or the crack of machine-gun bullets, at any moment. There were no sounds except the splashes of our paddles and our own frantic heavy breathing. Suddenly the boat scraped bottom. We had reached the far shore safely.

When we disembarked in knee-deep water, a hoarse voice commanded us, "Climb over the bank and assemble behind the white house next to the road."

It didn't take long for more boatloads of HQ personnel to reach the north bank and assemble. I heard Jessie James calling for Tibor. Jessie was now the S-3 officer with responsibility for planning and operations for the battalion. There was a whispered conference over a map by the light of a raincoat-shielded flashlight's glow. Then Tibor called to me.

"We're going to lead the battalion from this bridgehead," he said. "Follow along the road eastward to a canal, then follow the canal until we come to a bridge. We'll check it out if it's still standing."

The battalion was to then cross over the bridge and secure the ground just to the east of the canal against a flank attack.

By now, it was pitch dark. We really missed the artificial moonlight that the searchlights had provided in the mountains. Tibor and I groped our way along the road for what seemed forever but was probably just a few hundred yards, then turned north along the canal's banks. We walked with toes tentatively feeling for the fatal prongs of mines, and hand propelled in an exaggerated gentle swimming motion feeling for trip wires. The stark outline of a steel bridge appeared faintly over the canal's waters. It appeared to be intact. Tibor halted and hissed for Lieutenant James, who then told us to check it out.

Tibor dropped to his hands and knees and motioned for me to do likewise. Side by side, we began crawling across the steel-plated roadbed, on our hands and knees, gingerly feeling ahead for the trip wires of booby traps or mines. After twenty or thirty feet, the unforgiving sharp edges of the steel plates became excruciatingly painful. I wasn't too surprised when Tibor stood up and whispered, "Fuck it. I'm going to walk like a man. And if I'm meant to die here, so be it."

So the two of us walked, albeit gingerly, half-crouched, to the end of the span.

Once across, we ducked underneath, feeling for wires that may have led to demolition charges. None. I went back and told Jessie that all was clear. Then Tibor and I led the battalion to our assigned defensive area, near a hamlet called Sachetta. I again was called on to disperse the company in a perimeter defense and was about to crawl into a barn to sleep when Tibor called me over. He pointed south toward the river a few hundred yards away.

"E Company is down there somewhere," he said. "Go dig in with them and keep an eye out."

In half an hour I had fallen in with a platoon that identified itself as E Company, informed them of my mission, and instructed them to wake me if necessary. I scratched out a shallow trench and fell fast asleep. In the darkness they couldn't tell if I was a general or a corporal, but they didn't question my authority.

The crash of artillery shook me awake. It was dawn, and I hurriedly began to deepen my hole in anticipation of the German counterattack. I could see the shells exploding along the riverbank, a hundred or so yards away. I quickly plotted a route back to battalion HQ to inform the others if the attack really developed. In a few minutes the E Company commander, Captain Hammer, came running over and announced, "Don't worry about the shellfire. It's our own."

*Great!* The inference was that we were impervious to our own artillery. We knew better and kept our heads down. The shelling was, in fact, from the 85th Infantry Division, unaware of our presence across the river. The artillery was softening up the area for their river crossing. The shelling soon stopped, and I walked back to the CP and told Tibor that if we were counterattacked from that direction, it would be our own Fifth Army.

While engineers threw a pontoon bridge across the Po, we spent a couple of days resting in the perimeter at the eastern edge. That meant we had access to vehicles again. As soon as a few tanks and trucks towing artillery joined us, we merged again into long columns marching north.

Nightfall brought us to the edge of an airfield near the town of Villa Franca south of Verona. Although I remained with the S-2 squad, I was ordered to resume my job as a battalion guide as well. After billeting the company in a nearby compound, I joined a boisterous crowd of GIs and Italians in a nearby bistro, from which we staggered completely looped a few hours later. Had the Germans chosen to counterattack that night, the war might have had a different end. Nobody at HQ bothered to post sentries; our company was safely in the center of the circled companies of the battalion.

ONE OF THE war's strangest tales developed at Villa Franca airfield that day, April 25. A German pilot, unaware that we had captured the field, brought his plane in for a landing. He was immediately surrounded. The 10th Mountain Division had captured its first German airplane.

At dawn a convoy of empty trucks roared into the courtyard of our compound. Still groggy from the booze-induced sleep, we mounted the trucks, grateful for the rest of our swollen feet. We again headed north through the edge of Verona, then northwest until early afternoon when we came to the shores of Lake Garda. The battalion fell into a column of companies behind us. Pete Cantine and I were summoned to a group of officers huddled on the road that skirted the lake's eastern shore.

Pointing at me, Jessie said, "You and Pete are to be the lead scouts. We will go through the 87th and attack to the north up the eastern shore of the lake. You and Pete get out ahead of the column…a mile or two…and report back to the lead company if you spot anything."

"Spot anything" can be translated as "get shot at."

Pete and I took off, attempting to reach the 87th Regiment to stop them so we could pass through. Unbeknownst to us, the regiment had turned off to the northeast and proceeded up the ridge of the mountains that defined the eastern boundary of the valley. Pete and I raced along the shore at break-neck speed (thanks again, Camp Swift), and reached the town of Malcesine just as darkness fell. We had covered nearly twenty miles on foot in less than six hours.

Footsore, weary, and discouraged about not catching up to the 87th, we decided to call it a day. We were at least a couple miles ahead of the rest of the battalion. We waited near the town square for the rest of the battalion to catch up, and when they didn't arrive, Pete started pounding on the door of what appeared to be a mansion. He yelled, *"Americani, Americani!"*

In moments, an upstairs shutter flew open and the jabbering face of a middle-aged woman appeared. In another moment, a man opened the front door and ran to us with open arms. Crying and hugging us, he dragged us inside and seated us at the dining room table. He produced a bottle of wine, rescued from the basement, which added to the welcome. The couple soon added cheese and bread to the table. Pete, who had a good working knowledge of pidgin-Italian, had them put some water on to boil in the kitchen. We plunged in our K-ration cans and enjoyed a warm meal.

That was only the beginning. More buckets of water were heated and soon the luxurious marble bathtubs upstairs were filled. Quilts and feather-filled mattresses on huge beds were offered for our use. Soon we were in the tubs, lolling about like ancient Romans. After toweling dry, we dropped into exhausted sleep, half-buried in the luxury of real feather beds. When we awoke at nearly noon, we found all of our clothes had been washed, dried before a blaze in the giant fireplace, and ironed

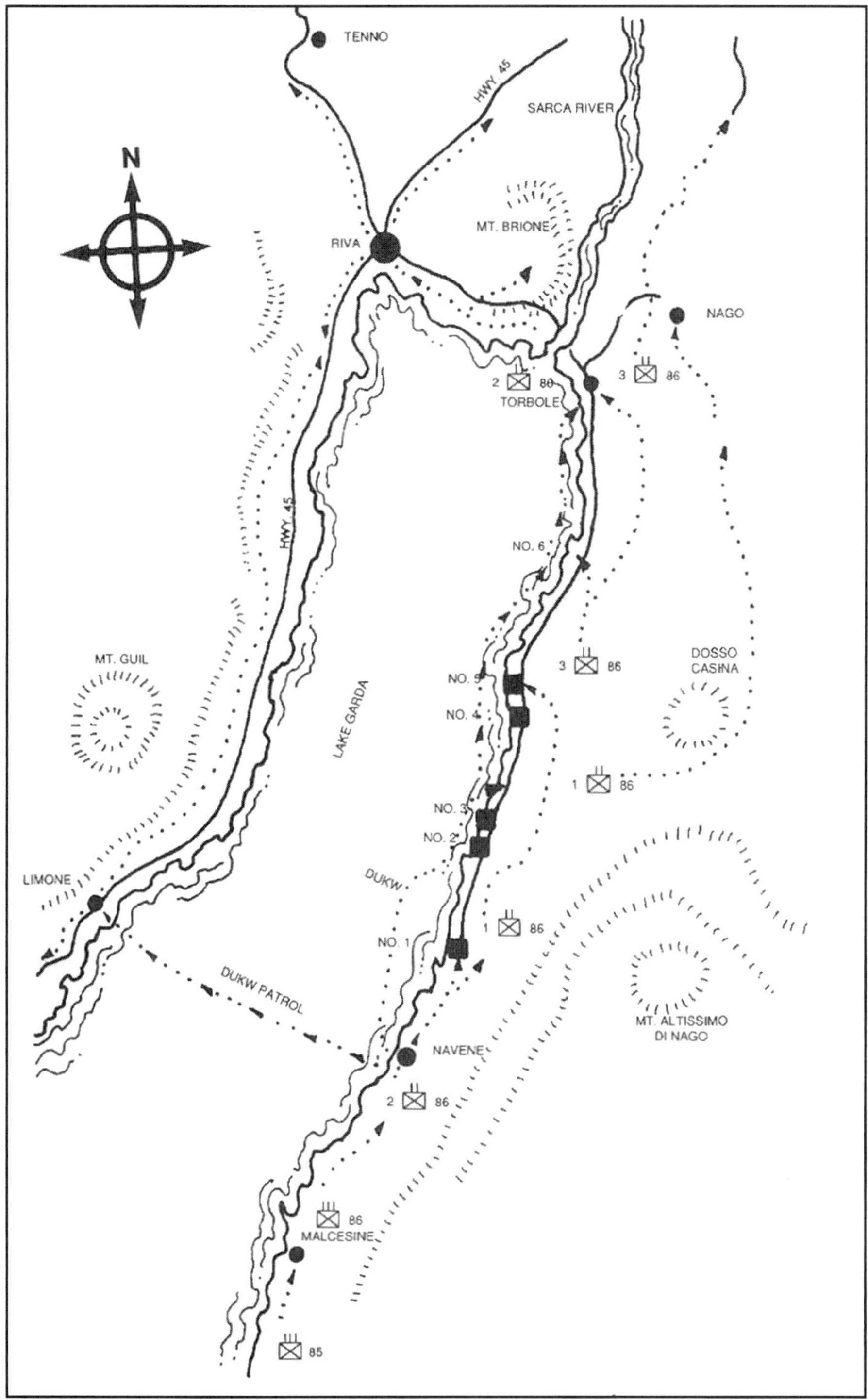


Route of the 10th—approaching northern end of Lake Garda (From *Soldiers on Skis*)

to perfection. Soon we were freshly shaved, doused in a pungent Italian perfume, and looking like we were in the midst of a furlough at the nearest whorehouse. Our hosts continued in their hospitality, supplementing our K-rations with a breakfast of eggs and toast.

Reluctantly, we investigated the persistent noise from outside the windows. Sure enough, the rest of the troops had arrived, after being passed through by the 86th. The men in our battalion rested by the side of the road, waiting assignments to a billet. We soon located the men of HQ Company and joined them in a shoreline hotel. The town of Malcesine was a lakeside resort, and there were enough beds to house a full division. We never did fully explain the circumstances of our pristine appearance to Tibor or anyone else. They thought we had stumbled into a local whorehouse, and had received the full treatment. Let 'em guess.

The hard fighting continued further up the coast, and stories of blown tunnels and enemy artillery barrages filtered down to us. The lack of usable roads made it difficult for our artillery to be brought up in close support of advancing infantry. Amphibious trucks known as DUKWs could carry the pack 75s, and a limited number of guns and crews were transported to Riva, at the north end of the lake. In an almost senseless tragedy, one DUKW was overloaded with men and a cannon and was swamped by rough water shortly after sailing. All but one man of the twenty-six aboard perished. (In the fall of 2004, an attempt to locate and raise the DUKW and recover the remains of those who drowned was made, but in vain.)

From the window of my hotel billet, I watched with astonishment as a British gun crew loaded its Long Tom 155 sideways onto an Italian sailboat. The barrel extended far over the gunwale of the port side and the tailpiece over the starboard as it left the dock at Malcesine. It took a genius at improvisation to think up that plan, and a very skilled boat crew to keep the boat from swamping.

The division then suffered a major tragedy. Colonel William Darby, the officer who had created and commanded the Rangers, and who became our assistant division commander after Brigadier General Robinson Duff was wounded during the drive across the Po Valley, was killed on April 30 when a random German shell exploded in the town square of Torbole, at the northern end of Lake Garda, where Darby and a few others were standing around.

I wrote to Lois on that same day: *"Rumors of peace have been flying around here thick and fast—we don't know what to believe anymore. Only one thing seems sure—in a matter of days, or perhaps only hours—this mess is over.... I'll never understand how man can destroy himself by such horrible means. Even more than I hate the krauts and Japs, I hate war."*

During the next few days, the rumors of peace turned into reality. When they were confirmed by the surrender of the German army in Italy on May 2, Pete, Dave Williams, Stan Nelson, and I celebrated by emptying rifles into a buoy floating in the lake just beyond the pier, tossing a few grenades into the lake, and emptying a bottle of vino that Stan had been saving for just that occasion. But the vino couldn't wash away the faces of those we lost. To this day, nothing can.

# 21: Peace Descends

The Germans in Italy surrendered on May 2, 1945, and the end of fighting in Italy was marked by an immediate return to garrison conditions. That meant shaving, haircuts, saluting all known to be officers, buttoning all buttons, and finding a laundry where uniforms could be washed and ironed. Cigarettes remained the currency of choice for all civilian-provided services. A full pack could buy almost anything and a carton equaled a fortune. Through some quirk of Army logic, I continued to be issued a full carton of Chelseas and Fleetwoods every week, even though our free cigarettes were supposed to stop when combat ceased.

Roadblocks were set up along the shore road to capture stray Germans and send them to POW enclosures. I was assigned as Sergeant of the Guard one day when we halted a southbound convoy of trucks with British markings. Since the tunnels were still blocked, they had to have taken a circuitous route over the mountains from the Adige River Valley. Jammed into the back were dozens of rag-clad men, some wearing stripes of German concentration-camp inmates. Their appearance was haunting, not much more than skin and bones, and they bore the vacant stares of tortured men. I telephoned Jessie to describe what I saw and heard him carry on a muffled conversation with someone. In a few moments, he said, "Let 'em pass."

A few years ago I read a book about the Jewish Brigade—Palestinian Jews who fought as part of the British Eighth Army. Their self-appointed postwar mission was to rescue survivors of the death camps, using trucks borrowed or stolen from their own units and bringing those people to camps in Italy, from which they could be secreted into Palestine. In some minor way, we helped those people who founded the state of Israel avoid months in a refugee camp.

In another incident that day, an Italian civilian came running to me crying (through a translator) that a GI had stolen his bicycle. He pointed to a GI sitting on a bike a few yards away. I asked the GI where he had obtained the bike and got a slew of evasive answers. The Italian, again through a translator, told me his initials were painted on the underside of the saddle. Sure enough, they were. I ordered the GI to relinquish the bike, which he did, but not before threatening to kill me. I pulled my captured P-38 pistol and invited him to try, but he slunk off muttering under his breath. Another GI who knew him told me he witnessed the stealing, and that I did the right thing. Two good deeds in one day.

The machine gun I had carried sporadically from the beginning of the final march had ended up in Harry's jeep after we crossed the Po. I did the final trek with my pistol and an M-3 sub-machine gun. As our equipment caught up with us, I was presented with my battered Garand to clean and refurbish, and with the belt-fed machine gun to clean and return to the supply room. The rifle presented no problem. Half an hour with a can of solvent, a can of oil, a few rags, some patches, and a toothbrush did the job. Except for a few scratches and dents in the stock, my rifle was as good as new.

I was less familiar with the workings of the .30-caliber machine gun and soon re-learned that to clear the gun of all ammo, it took two jerks on the operating handle, not just one. My first attempt, using only one, resulted in my blasting a round into a corner where the floor met a wall. Fortunately, the bullet ricocheted past my ear, off the ceiling, and finally hit the floor behind me. What irony it would have been to take a fatal bullet from my own friendly-fire accident just days after hostilities ceased.

The next day Tibor called me into the operations room. He announced that I was to be part of a battalion task force whose mission was to seal the Italian-Austrian border. We were to prevent the surrendering German troops from slipping into Austria where fighting was still in progress. Eight of us from HQ, carrying a week's rations, mounted two jeeps with our rucksacks loaded into two trailers. I carried my M-1, the P-38, and two bandoliers of ammo. The others were similarly armed or carried carbines. Bob Fels, as operations sergeant, was the senior non-com. Lieutenant Ryan, our new S-2, was the officer in charge of us and a few line company riflemen, who were to be our security.

We would lead a platoon-sized convoy to a German Army HQ hidden deep in the mountains. The Germans there were to plot the location of their main units on the maps Bob carried. Then we were to travel to a German Corps HQ to enforce their surrender. Once we arrived at the tri-corner border, the line company platoon would man checkpoints to prevent stragglers from moving north.

I felt like a sacrificial goat. With a handful of light arms, we were supposed to make sure that several German divisions observed the terms of their surrender. I don't recall that we had any radio powerful enough to send an SOS back to Malcesine if needed, but would depend instead on the good will of the local German commander.

For several hours our entourage crept up snaking narrow roads carved from sheer cliffs. Tunnels pierced the rock outcroppings where there was insufficient room to construct a cliff-side road. The adjacent drop-offs were a chilling thousand feet to canyon floors. One miscalculation on a curve and we might never have been found.

Finally, we reached a castle set high on a ridge in a spectacular setting. We parked in the courtyard, and Lieutenant Ryan, Bob Fels, and our German-born American translator went inside to procure the information they needed. The rest of us were left to guard the jeeps from several hundred German troops who smilingly surrounded us and asked us to pose for pictures. They gratefully traded their vile Turkish cigarettes for our American ones. Unfortunately, not one spoke English and none of us knew a word of German, so conversations were extremely limited. They showed extraordinary curiosity about our jeeps. In halting pidgin English and Italian, we finally figured out that they were asking, "How far can it go on a tank of fuel?"

Well, math was never my strong point, and you can imagine how screwed up my answer was when I tried to translate "miles per gallon" into the equivalent "kilometers per liter." Their gasps and raised eyebrows convinced me that my solution to that mathematical problem was a bit optimistic.

Soon thereafter, we were en route again, dropping into the valley and passing through Trento, where several hundred wounded and captured GIs waved to us

German troops surrendered to us by the thousands in April and May 1945.

(Author photo)

A dreaded German "88" abandoned along the side of a road because its prime mover (right) had run out of fuel. To appreciate the size of this gun, note the Italian girl (left) standing under the barrel.

(Author photo)

frantically from a roadside hospital. To them, we were the armor-clad knights on horseback who rode to their rescue. We continued non-stop to Bolzano, thence turned westward until we reached the little city of Silandro, near the Swiss, Austrian, and Italian borders. The line company platoon continued on to the border where they would maintain the checkpoint.

We parked in front of a main street hotel while Lieutenant Ryan and our translator went inside to make arrangements for our billet. An irresistible aroma wafted our way from a bakery across the street. We followed our noses into the shop and were greeted by hostile stares from the customers and the baker. What had been omitted from our pre-departure briefing was the historical background of this area: It was ethnically German. The territory had been taken from Austria at the conclusion of World War I and made a part of Italy, and we were NOT welcome liberators. By gesture, I picked out a slew of fancy-looking pastries and a few loaves of bread and generously offered a handful of Occupation Currency, now the legal tender in all of Italy. The suspicious proprietor fingered it nervously, held it up to the light, shook his head, and tried to hand it back. He was obviously unfamiliar with the new Italian Lira notes.

*"Gut, gut,"* I said. The proprietor continued to protest until I ended the argument

An American M-3 Stuart light tank. The 10th had no "organic" armor, so this one was probably a reconnaissance tank from the 751st Tank Battalion that provided armored support for us throughout the Italian campaign.

(U.S. Army photo)

by slowly raising the muzzle of my rifle. The baker shrugged his shoulders and stuck the bills in his cash drawer.

We then checked into the hotel by unrolling our sleeping bags on the floor of a bed-less room. We left one jeep crew to guard our equipment, while four of us took off in the other jeep for the castle at the edge of town, which had been designated to us as German HQ. We drove into a huge courtyard past the watchful eyes of two German soldiers who were guarding stacks of German rifles and rows of machine guns. The German officer in charge was summoned and through our interpreter was told by Lieutenant Ryan that all officers were to add their sidearms to the stacks of rifles. The German officer vigorously protested that it would be impossible for him to maintain order and discipline without sidearms. Lieutenant Ryan told him to follow orders or else, and that we would return in the morning to see that it was done. We then returned to the hotel and enjoyed a weird banquet of C-rations topped off with the exquisite German pastries. Then to sleep, taking turns staying awake as guards for the jeeps and trailers.

Shortly after daybreak, we were again parked in the courtyard of the castle where the unhappy German officer kept protesting that he needed more time to gather all the sidearms. His troops were scattered, he explained. He did not have gasoline and it would take all day to assemble the horse-drawn wagons that were dispatched to retrieve the pistols.

"Okay," said the lieutenant. "One more day."

As we drove back to the hotel, an excited Italian hailed us and in broken English informed us that several SS men were holed up in a ski lodge at Monte Civedale, a few miles away. The lieutenant decided that capturing SS men was part of our mission, so shortly after noon Lieutenant Ryan, Bob Fels, our driver, and I set off on the adventure—jeep, trailer, and all.

It took less than two hours to navigate the agonizing, winding trail to the lodge, which we spotted just at tree line at the foot of a glacier. We parked in the trees, and in teams of two crept up to the lodge from opposite directions. There, we were greeted by an old woman and two unarmed men in civilian clothes. In broken English, and responding to Bob's Yiddish, the men acknowledged that they were, indeed, in the SS. They had tried to avoid capture, fearing they would be turned over to the Russians. Both men's homes were in the areas already occupied by the Russians, and repatriation there was a feared fate. They accepted with relief our assurance they would be sent to an American POW camp.

As darkness began to descend, we decided that navigating down the precipitous mountain road at night would be foolish. Instead, we would spend the night at the lodge and leave in the morning. Lieutenant Ryan quietly instructed the driver to disable the jeep by removing and pocketing the distributor rotor, and we "checked" into the lodge.

It was an interesting night. The old woman, who turned out to be the caretaker, heated our C-rations for dinner and found some extras for our prisoners. She broke out a few bottles of wine and the seven of us boisterously celebrated the war's end in the lodge's cozy dining room. Bob Fel's knowledge of Yiddish served to translate enough German to make conversation. The main thrust of the SS men's questions centered on how soon we would become allies in the fight against the Russians. The Germans always felt that we should be Russia's enemy, just as they were, and couldn't understand why we were Stalin's ally.

The two prisoners seemed less dangerous dressed as civilians, so we all retired to comfortable accommodations after dinner for a good night's sleep—a rare night on a comfortable bed. It seemed ludicrous to even think about posting a guard. (Luckily, that proved unnecessary.) Nevertheless, I locked my door, propped a chair under the handle, and slept with my P-38 under my pillow.

The caretaker's gentle rap on the door awakened me in the morning. After a breakfast of C-rations, Bob and one of our German prisoners found skis and boots in the lodge's ski shop and took off for a few runs down the glacier. I felt less confident of my ski legs but found the necessary equipment and managed a few solo runs on what was probably the beginner's slope just above the lodge. Clearly, my Camp Hale expertise had dissipated as I spent an inordinate amount of time trying to regain my feet.

A brochure printed in 1937 showing the ski resort at Civedale where we took two hiding SS men into custody—after we dined and skied with them.

(Provided by the author)

By mid-morning, we had re-packed the trailer, made room for our prisoners, and took off down the mountain. At a cluster of houses just above the valley floor, an Italian halted us with information about a wounded German soldier being cared for at a nearby house. Obviously, the Italians who had been moved into this ethnically German area under pressure from Mussolini, and treated as second-class citizens, were bent on getting their revenge. We checked the house and sure enough, a bandaged, semi-conscious German soldier occupied one of the beds. We decided he was too badly hurt to be moved and chose instead to simply report his whereabouts to the German commander. Back in Silandro, we turned the two SS prisoners over to the Germans and returned to the billet for the night.

Early the next morning, we were relieved of our mission by troops from another unit and were given orders to return to Malcesine. I was puzzled by Lieutenant Ryan's orders to detour to the German HQ. We pulled into the courtyard of the castle and relaxed while Lieutenant Ryan and the translator entered the building. In a few minutes, out they came with a German officer who directed some of his troops to load an enormous pile of pistols into our trailer. Lieutenant Ryan went to the rifle stacks, examined one carefully, and added the souvenir to our trailer load. When that was done, we piled back into the jeeps and took off.

A few miles out of town, the lieutenant ordered the drivers to pull off the road and park in a stand of trees. Under his direction, a blanket was spread on the ground and onto it all the pistols were unloaded. We sat in a circle around the blanket, and Lieutenant Ryan offered them as souvenirs. We took turns, one by one, and I ended up with nearly twenty guns that I stuffed into my unrolled sleeping bag. We then resumed the journey back to Lake Garda, stopping for rations and gasoline at an ordnance company camped in the valley near Trento. While we ate, one of their men described over and over again the horrors of combat endured by his non-combatant ordnance company. It seemed they had been strafed once and lost a truck. I guess *horrors* are always *compared to what.*

When we pulled into Malcesine and word spread that I had a haul of pistols, Tibor suggested, using a tone of voice that permitted no dissent, that I keep one for myself and let the rest of the S-2 squad and company share the balance. Fair enough. I picked out a mint-condition Luger and the rest were quickly gobbled up. Lieutenant Ryan didn't stay with our company very long, but his reputation for fairness and as an expert requisitioner was well established. He later had his purloined Mauser rifle modified into a fine hunting rifle.

## 22: Occupation Duties

About a week later I was sent, alone, scurrying to a villa that overlooked the airport at Brescia. "Villa" may be an understatement; "castle" is a better description. All the doors were huge, at least ten feet high, inlaid with panes of stained glass worthy of a cathedral. The floors were gorgeous marble. The walls were adorned with magnificent frescoes and tapestries, and portraits of what must have been the ancient ancestors of the present owners covered the remaining space in profusion.

The view from the front steps was awesome in a different way. In a huge field nearby was an encampment of thousands, maybe tens of thousands, German prisoners. Some were lucky enough to be housed in tents they had salvaged; others just

The beautiful castle at Malcesine on Lake Garda where I was when the war in Europe ended. The castle was filled with German radio equipment—and a nice Italian couple who kept us clean and well fed.

(Provided by author)

stretched out on the grass. It appeared that our battalion was to assume guarding them while they were being processed to be sent home. Except for the huge entry hall and one other downstairs room, both devoid of furniture, the magnificent carved doors were locked to protect their contents. I spent most of the day stretched out on my butt on the cold floor.

Bob Fels and a few other HQ people drifted in and set up a temporary battalion headquarters. That night Bob scrounged up a ride for the two of us and we ended up in a bar in downtown Brescia. Bob immediately struck up a sign-language conversation with a pretty young Italian girl, and I used some discretion in drifting away. They waved to me from the door as they left.

I managed to find the truck driver who had given us the lift to Brescia, and with no other prospects on the horizon, we headed back to the villa. Bob returned the next day with a skeletal story of his romance. He would only relate that the young *signorina* insisted he use a *gomma*, a condom, because she did not want to have a *bambino*.

I spent a miserable night sleeping on the cold marble floor and was grateful when, early the next day, we were picked up by a truck crammed with HQ personnel and turned east. The 6x6 was so overloaded with men and equipment there was only room to stand. We made one brief stop to wolf down some rations and relieve ourselves of what the constantly jarred kidneys produced.

This time the rumors we had been hearing were right. Tito and his Communist Yugoslavian Army were making threats toward seizing Trieste and the adjacent area. The 10th was to occupy some of the land that he had threatened and prevent his conquest of this erstwhile Italian soil.

We rode for hours until we reached the outskirts of a little town named Trecesimo, a few miles north of Udine. We debouched onto what looked like a decent field for camping and, for the first time in Italy, were issued the standard two-man pup tents. Not the magnificent waterproof floored mountain tents which offered mosquito-proof netting at the door but the miserable, two-piece canvas job misnamed shelter halves, which were inadequate for any real shelter. We lined them up in exact rows with alignment confirmed by rope stretched from one end of a row to the other. Peacetime tactics to a fault.

The next day, rainfall made us realize that we were encamped on a flood plain. Within minutes, rivulets of water were trickling under the tents. Soon the trickles turned into raging torrents. We gathered rocks from the adjacent shores of the stream and built piles on which we could stow our gear above waterline. The tactic was ineffective, and that night I slept under a wet quilt. Stretched out on the tent in the sunshine, it had barely dried the next day before another storm came along and made for another miserable night. Finally, the brass moved us into town and into secure, waterproof billets. HQ was set up in the sample rooms of a furniture store, which had been emptied of all usable chairs, tables, and beds. The furniture had been moved to the second floor, which was placed off limits to the troops but kept open for the officers. Rank did have its privileges. The other companies of the battalion were scattered around town in such a way as to not interfere with the daily routine of our so-called Italian co-belligerents. Sleeping on the marble floor without the benefit of a mattress was not an easy chore, but it sure beat camping on a flood plain.

GARRISON DUTY HIT us with a vengeance. Combat boots had to be shined with pant legs neatly tucked into the top of our boots. Wrinkled or dirty clothing was not tolerated, and all buttons had to be properly fastened. Hats or helmets were mandatory, depending on daily assignments, and "Sir" was uttered with more frequency, even though we could occasionally slip into using first names for ranks below major and not bring down the roof.

The S-2 squad was given the assignment of daily jeep patrols to keep tabs on the activity of known Communist partisan groups, and to be sure they were not responsible for any unacceptable violence. Permissible violence included shaving the heads of women who had consorted with the Germans. Bald-headed women were not exactly commonplace, but they weren't a rarity, either. I wondered what fate would befall any woman who cottoned up to *us*.

To the casual observer, patrols were armed, of course. I carried my captured Walther P-38 pistol, loaded, and my M-1. Ammunition for the M-1 had supposedly been turned in, but I hid a few clips in my rucksack and slipped one in my rifle when I was patrolling. Some brass up the line had decided that if an incident occurred, it was okay for a few unarmed GIs to get murdered rather than risk a confrontation with the Yugoslavians or partisans.

While on patrol, we had spotted a country inn and made it a favorite stop for lunch on several occasions. A light touch of *da vino* with lunch made the monotony of K- and C-rations bearable. We arranged to have a banquet there one weekend night and bought some chickens for the event. "Buy" meant trading a few cartons of cigarettes to a nearby farmer. The meal was well prepared, and the S-2 squad left the inn that night thoroughly stuffed.

By the way, do you know how to make an Italian omelet? First, you steal two eggs....

Since the Table of Organization did not include me in its ranks, the S-2 squad was permitted to add one more member. The slot went to Hans W. Aschaffenburg, an arrogant, Austrian-born math genius who graduated from MIT in 1942 and later ended up as an Ivy League college professor. Hans was a stickler in seeking comfort and the blessings of civilization for himself and complained bitterly that his favorite toothpaste was impossible to find in the PX rations. He hinted that I would be judged a total failure as a non-com if I were unable to provide such a simple necessity for my squad. I consulted briefly with the battalion surgeon, who advised me that table salt would be a perfectly suitable substitute. The mess sergeant provided a small bag for use by the squad. Hans gave me a grumbling, half-assed thanks and let the subject drop.

Somewhere along the line, Hans had managed to illicitly acquire a pre-war Mercedes as his version of war loot. Pretty hotsy-totsy for a PFC. In his judgment no one knew how to build cars except the Germans, and he vowed to somehow get it home to the States. He kept it hidden in a garage near our HQ. When off duty, he foraged a few gallons of gasoline and took me for a ride in the mountains nearby more than once and drove around mountain curves at a madman's pace to demonstrate what a great handling car it was. Word of his acquisition somehow drifted up the ranks. He was confronted by our new battalion CO and was told he would have to give it up to the higher rank.

I've heard two versions of that story's conclusion: One is that Hans took the car to the edge of a mountain precipice, engaged the running engine into gear, jumped out, and let the car disappear over the edge of the cliff. The other is that some ingenious officer got the Mercedes into the hold of the ship that brought us home and had it unloaded at night at Camp Shanks, New York, where we disembarked, and became the proud possessor of Hans' pride and joy. I've never been able to verify either story.

JACK, (I USE a fictitious name here for the obvious reason of protecting a friend) came to me one afternoon with an intriguing offer. In a nearby three-house village, he had befriended an Italian family that was totally bereft of male members. It included a toothless, ancient mother but more particularly her two daughters, both in their thirties. They had recently been shorn of their luxurious black hair. Local partisans accused them of consorting with the Germans and without benefit of trial, their punishment had been meted out. Jack's girlfriend, the older sister, was a longtime widow.

The younger one, whom I was to befriend, was married, but her husband was a prisoner of war. He had been captured in North Africa and was presently imprisoned in a camp in the United States. Both women were childless. Jack had become their resource of a daily ration of a few cans of food, thanks to the cooperation of the mess sergeant, LePore, who couldn't stand the thought of fellow Italians starving. Their current benefactor, besides Jack, was a British artillery non-com, but his unit was about to be moved. Jack was soliciting me to become the Brit's replacement.

Jack flat-out promised that the reward for my cooperation had romantic overtones. With an offer of additional rations from the mess sergeant, I reluctantly agreed to the opportunity.

The next night, with a couple cans of beans stuck in our pockets and a loaf of bread under my arm, Jack and I hiked over moonlit roads and fields to the little cluster of houses where the family lived. The women both appeared to be clean, well groomed, and decently attractive. Jack made the introduction in pidgin Italian, and Maria greeted me with a smile and a warm hug. The women gratefully accepted our gifts and, giggling, led us out the door and up a nearby trail, each of them carrying a rolled-up blanket. Mama giggled as we left.

Perhaps fifty yards up a gentle knoll, Maria pulled me off the trail and spread the blanket while Jack and her sister continued ahead and disappeared over a little knoll. In an instant Maria shed her dress, revealing a lithe torso, and she was frantically getting me out of my clothes. She overcame my inexperience with an expert touch and—too quickly—I was left panting and exhausted on the blanket. The rest of the story would make an interesting pornographic novel.

This scene was to be repeated nearly every night for the next several weeks, always followed by the precaution of a stop at the aid station for a prophylactic preventative treatment. The on-duty medic and I became fast friends despite his oft-expressed jealousy.

It belatedly occurred to me that no birth control method was being used and I wondered what would happen if she became pregnant. I posed that question to her in broken Italian one night, and she blandly answered that she would say I raped her.

To say I was shocked is an understatement. I broke into a cold sweat. Rape was a capital offense. I told Jack what had happened, and that as far as I was concerned, the affair was over. He could go it alone or find someone else to be Maria's friend. A few days later, Maria showed up outside the open window of my billet and called my name. I hid while one of the guys told her I had been transferred back to the States. A suspicious Maria hovered around the window of my billet for another week, but I managed to stay out of sight. Close call!

# 23: Gross Glockner

For several weeks thereafter, life became a total bore. Passes were issued to visit Venice, but most of my meager pay went home to be banked, and I didn't have the funds to handle that kind of a weekend. I chose instead to improve my language skills by enrolling in an Italian class. Even that became a drag. A variety of other schools were started to give us some off-duty activities while we awaited re-deployment to the Pacific to help finish off the war against Japan. One of the announced classes was to be a glacier-climbing class at Gross Glockner Glacier in Austria. I had lost interest in my Italian class, and my name was one of the first submitted to hit the ice. Besides, it was getting difficult to avoid Maria.

In no time I was one of a handful of men from the battalion en route over an obscure pass into Austria, through Linz, and on to Gross Glockner. Parked in fields along the route were hundreds of German tanks rendered helpless by the lack of fuel. That was at least one way the Air Force had saved lives. The bombers' destruction of German oil sources at Ploesti, Romania, had emasculated their armored divisions, which could have made an enormous difference in the final battles.

We arrived at Gross Glockner Glacier, skirting the wall of ice that formed its end. The huge mass of iced moved sullenly downhill a few feet a year. Snow that had fallen centuries ago became gradually exposed and slowly melted from the shrinking glacier. We later heard stories about the bodies of men, who had fallen into crevices hundreds of years ago, suddenly reappearing, preserved by the ice, but now freed from their frozen tombs. I didn't see any during my brief sojourn there.

Set on huge rocks bordering the ice mass, the glacier-climbing school occupied what had been a German Army barracks. They were comfortable enough but not a match for the huge tourist facility towering above us on the shoulder of the mountain facing Gross Glockner. Of course we investigated it, but the facility was securely locked and boarded up. As if to attract a casual passerby, a shelf adjacent to the door held pamphlets advertising its facilities and prices. In peaceful prewar days, I could have enjoyed dinner for three marks or a room with running water for seven marks.

The glacier-climbing school at Gross Glockner. The strange-looking vehicle in the foreground is a half-tracked German motorcycle known as a *Kraftkettenrad.*

(Author photo)

The next week was fully involved in learning about the ice-climbing equipment as we clambered across the jagged glacier and learned to manage the risks of deep crevices. We learned to respect the weird moans and thunderous noises accompanying the glacier's slow journey down the valley. We spent hours learning how to use ice axes to cut steps in the ice cliffs and how to climb almost vertical walls of ice using crampons (iron spikes which fit over our boots). The rope work was a repeat of what we had learned in our rock-climbing classes at Camp Hale, and I managed to arm myself with the needed equipment from abandoned Italian and German stores. I even found a pair of Italian boots in my size, fitted with soles of metal studs for a secure grip on rock and ice. The final test was the climb of Gross Glockner itself, which was a relatively easy climb to a hut on the ridge, followed by an assault on the peak.

We were deprived of the luxury of a kitchen crew in the camp, so we had to manage on C- and K-rations supplemented by raw onions that we ate as if they were apples. All of us stunk so badly by the lack of bathing facilities that no one paid heed to the wafting and persistent odor of onions. As we neared the end of the school term, the thought of returning to the boredom of Trecesimo overcame me. The threat of pursuit by Maria added to my reluctance to leave Gross Glockner. I wrote a note to the first sergeant, asking permission to stay another week. It went back on the ration truck, and his answer accompanied its return with more K-rations and the few stragglers who made up the next class. I was permitted to stay for another round. I could remain forever as long as I stayed out of trouble.

As a "grad student," I was permitted to be a junior assistant instructor to one of the experts and had a ball just showing off my newly acquired skills to a bunch of tyros. I chose to skip their graduation exercise (another climb of the mountain) and instead watched their progress through binoculars. As I sat on a huge boulder watching their plodding approach to the hut on the ridge, I chose that moment to write Lois and, as I had initially done while on furlough in Chicago, ask her hand in marriage, the wedding to take place when I got home. That, of course, would be some time in the future. We still had to win the war against Japan.

As I sealed the letter, a truck and a jeep appeared. They carried news that we were to report to an assembly area in Florence immediately. We were to head home for a brief furlough prior to re-deployment. One of the instructors raced across the glacier and up the mountain to retrieve the class while the rest of us began to pack our gear.

A few hours later, I was perched in the back seat of the jeep as we headed south toward Florence. We took two days to make the trip, stopping en route to celebrate our departure from Italy by getting roaring drunk in a small town *albergo*. We were well hung over when we found the staging area camp on the banks of the Arno River and rejoined our respective companies. My friend Tibor had seen to it that the barracks bag containing the clothing and equipment I had left in Trecesimo was packed and waiting for me on a bunk. In a few days we would be homeward bound.

## 24: Homeward Bound

The sojourn at Florence wasn't long, but it was marked by a few events that may have affected my future. The first thing I did was refuse a promotion.

Our battalion sergeant major, Dutch DePodwin, was promoted to the equivalent position at regiment, and I was offered his job. That would have entailed a promotion to master sergeant, with six stripes, and a huge increase in pay and status. I might have been tempted to stay in service, and that would have put me in the line of fire when the Korean War began a few years later. It might also have affected my relationship with Lois, who might have viewed life as an Army wife with disdain.

On an immediate basis, it meant transfer again out of the S-2 squad into a clerical position, and a closer relationship to our company commander, for whom I had no particular respect or admiration. He struck me, perhaps unfairly, as just another wheeler-dealer, not really concerned about the welfare of the men in our company. I explained my feelings to Tibor, who I would have then outranked. He agreed with my decision, as did Jessie, whom I think bore no great love for Shep's successor either. I was comfortable with Lieutenant Ryan, the S-2 officer, who kept pretty much to himself and did not pose a threat through ineptitude to the remaining friends I had in the squad. I told our battalion commander, Lieutenant Colonel Seiss E. Wagner, from whom the promotion offer originated, that I preferred to stay where I was as battalion guide and assistant S-2 squad leader, and thanked him for the consideration.

Another job came my way through Tibor and this one I accepted. He was asked to put a staff together for a 2nd Battalion newspaper. Although the only writing background I had was writing letters to Lois, I accepted the position as writer of "The Man on the Street" column. When we left Florence bound for Naples by train a few days later, I was mentally preparing the first questions I would pose to men in the battalion.

"What's the second thing you're going to do when you get home?" I asked Barney Dexter, my first interviewee. He set the stage with his response:

"There isn't going to be any second thing. I'm going to first thing myself to death."

HEADING FOR HOME did not yet entail a hope for discharge and civilian life. It meant a few weeks furlough and then re-embarkment to finish off the Japanese. We didn't relish the thought but accepted the necessity.

We disembarked the train in Naples and were trucked to the empty rooms of an Italian university dormitory. More cold marble floors on which to sleep. It did have an adjacent Olympic-size swimming pool filled with near-freezing mountain stream water, but it was a welcome diversion. Art expert Bob Fels took me in tow again, this time for a tour of the Naples Art Museum and lectures on the advantages of knowledge of human anatomy for the sculptor. He marveled at the accurate depiction of every muscle in the human body in several sculptures. I just enjoyed the female statues.

The whores of Naples were regularly pimped by their younger brothers and sisters. My friend Sergeant W., though happily married, feared he'd forgotten the basics and sought to refresh his memory at the expense of only a carton of cigarettes. Tempted by a youngster bragging about the talents of his teenaged sister, Sergeant W. was escorted to their home—a cave carved into one of the Napoli's cliffs. Inside, the mother of the two scooted herself and the young pimp out to afford the loving couple some privacy.

Before W. had finished his refresher course, the faint smell of something burning had burgeoned into a thick cloud of smoke. The young whore yelled for mama, who came charging back into the cave to remove a boiled-over and charred pot of pasta. Sergeant W. never did complete his re-education, nor did he get a refund for services not rendered.

The benefits of being a member of the media came fully to light as soon as we boarded the *Marine Fox* for home. The ship was a Victory Ship version of a troop carrier, with bunks stacked like cordwood six high in the bowels of the hold. The newspaper staff was given deluxe quarters on the deck immediately below the top deck and issued cots with mattresses. Best of all, we were assigned to eat with the ship's crew, which meant real meals served on real dishes, three times a day, instead of the unrecognizable glop slopped into mess kits. We actually had pancakes, eggs, and bacon cooked to order every breakfast, and steak every night—topped off with ice cream for dessert.

My innocuous column appeared in every mimeographed issue of the ship's paper until, several days out to sea, two events shook us out of our torpor.

First came the astonishing news that a bomber had accidentally flown into the

Empire State Building (a forerunner of 9/11?).* We got the news over the ship's radio and embellished the bare facts as best we could with a special issue.

The second piece of news was the dropping of the atomic bomb on Japan on August 6, 1945. In a script I wrote for a newscast to be read over the ship's PA system, I described Japan as being locked in a gigantic cannonball about to explode. The exploding A-bombs dropped over Hiroshima and Nagasaki brought about riotous joy and speculation that war would be over before we landed on Japanese beaches. By the time we sailed into New York harbor, hostilities had already ceased.

Our ship was greeted by crowds of cheering people along the banks of the Hudson, by ferries and other craft blasting their whistles in salute, and by fireboats' hoses shooting streams of water in the air. We lined the decks of the *Marine Fox* as she sailed triumphantly past the Statue of Liberty and under the George Washington Bridge, thence past West Point to Camp Shanks on the Hudson's western bank.

With just a bit of poetic license, I have aggravated my wife by relating my disembarkation from the ship. As I tell it, there was a pay phone on the dock, and I ran to it and placed a collect call to my father's office in Chicago.

"Congratulations," he said. "You're getting married next week."

"To whom?" I asked. (Lois hates the joke.)

Lois had received my letter proposing marriage, by which I meant when the war was over. She assumed otherwise. The news of our disembarking from Italy had made the local Chicago paper, and after estimating the date of my arrival, Lois and our families had planned the wedding. I went through the processing for the furlough, oblivious of the life-changing plans being made.

Several of those living in the New York area took advantage of lax controls and scooted home for the first weekend. I was tempted to visit Johnny and Ned's families, both of whom lived nearby, but the guilt of surviving was already taking its toll. I decided I couldn't face them. I instead spent a quiet few days, took in some movies, and just tried to adjust to the thought of being a civilian again. The GI Bill had been explained to us aboard ship by an earnest Special Services soldier. College was definitely in my plans, but I wasn't really sure what field I would pursue.

Processing for the anticipated furlough began with discarding the old uniforms and laying all equipment, including war booty, on the bed. My Luger and P-38 were legitimate souvenirs, as were my ice axe, Italian mountain boots, carabineers, and pitons. But the German Schmeisser burp gun, a fully automatic 9mm sub-machine gun that I had secreted in my barracks bag, was a no-no. Cleverly, I tied a string to the handle and shoved it as far as I could into the ceiling heater vent. I

* On the foggy, drizzly morning of July 28, 1945, an Army B-25 bomber, lost in the low clouds over Manhattan, crashed into the 79th floor of the Empire State Building, killing the three men aboard the plane and eleven civilians in the building.

could retrieve it when the inspection for illegal booty was over. I confidently went for a shower and clean uniform.

When I returned I was stunned to learn that I wasn't as smart as I thought. My little stunt had been anticipated and the burp gun was gone. To whom could I complain?

In a few days, those of us from the Chicago area were packed onto a train headed for Camp Grant, from where it all began, and from which we would be issued our furloughs. The paperwork took only a day after our arrival. I called my dad to tell him I would be home the next day, then immediately boarded the Illinois Central train to Chicago. I walked into the trembling arms of my surprised father in his office. He examined me thoroughly to make sure all the fingers and toes were there, and we wept with joy.

A cab ride (freebie by a grateful cabbie) brought me to our family's apartment. Lois, who had moved in permanently when my brother joined the Navy, was still asleep. She still may think she dreamed the whole homecoming.

WITHIN TEN DAYS we were married and life began anew.

Getting the wedding party assembled was a chore. Among all my friends, I was the first one home from the war. My brother was available to be best man, but aside from one 4-F friend, the ushers included several strangers and one 10th Mountain medic, Ken Hanson, whose patch my father recognized on the street, and whom he literally kidnapped to stand up for me. Ken, as it turned out, was in my company and was a welcome addition.

Although my brother made all the post-wedding hotel arrangements for us, he spared us the usual practical jokes, and we retired in safety to a downtown Chicago hotel. Instead of the reserved honeymoon suite, we were lucky, in the pervasive wartime atmosphere, to get a room at all, and this one had unnecessary twin beds. When we checked out the following morning, the maid noted that only one had been occupied and tossed off a quip, "You must be honeymooners." How true.

The honeymoon week was spent at the rustic lodge of Starved Rock State Park, a haven for other GI honeymooners, seventy-five miles southwest of Chicago on the Illinois River. My marital joy there was expressed by singing in the shower. Unknown to me, the hotel's ventilation system was shared by every room in that wing, and my singing was carried everywhere. I silently blushed when the breakfast conversation with the other guests pondered the source of the music. (Five years later, I took a Boy Scout troop to Starved Rock State Park on a winter camping trip and taught them rock climbing. And fifty years later, one of those Boy Scouts found me

Lois and me, photographed a few days before our wedding in 1945

(Author photo)

Our wedding day on August 25, 1945. The lovely bride wore white satin and lace. The groom wore olive-drab wool.

(Author photo)

and related that he became a CIA operative and used my rappelling technique out of a helicopter into Panama during a special operation.)

Back in Chicago, as my thirty-day furlough was coming to an end, a telegram from Sergeant Leisentreit granted me a two-week extension and, thanks to my father's generosity, Lois and I paid a visit to New York. I called Tibor and received an immediate invitation to visit him and his wife Madeleine and their infant daughter (who had been born at the moment we were jumping off in the Belvedere attack).

Madeleine had been house-sitting in the luxurious mansion of musical artist George M. Cohan. It sat on a hill with a beautiful view overlooking Long Island Sound.

She and Tibor were marvelous hosts. We also used the visit for a sightseeing spree that included the Staten Island Ferry, the Statue of Liberty, the Empire State Building, and Radio City Music Hall. My cousin Gladys (Harry Weinsaft's long-lost love) took us to a famous nightclub on Long Island, and we danced to the music of Harry James' orchestra.

But all good things come to an end. Ours did with a telegram from Sergeant Leisentreit, reminding me that the furlough was over and it was time to report to Camp Carson, Colorado. My new mother-in-law decided to make sure her only daughter would be properly housed in Colorado Springs and accompanied us to Colorado on her way back to California. We found initial housing as roomers with a very nice lady whose husband was in the far-off Pacific. That lasted only a couple weeks, when she got word of his impending return, and asked that we seek other quarters.

Following up on a newspaper ad, we landed in a tourist court aptly named Poor Boy Cabins. For some miserly sum, we got a cabin with a minuscule living room and a tiny kitchen but with a beautiful bedroom whose picture window featured Pike's Peak. And it was only a short bus ride from Camp Carson.

FOR THE FIRST few weeks, we were assigned to our original units and cheated on the prescribed training formats. When we had conditioning hikes scheduled, we marched to the nearest woods and hid there all day. I soon learned to stick a book in my back pocket to keep me occupied.

In November 1945, word came that the 10th was to be deactivated, and I was transferred to the base prison camp as a guard. Hundreds of German POWs were at the camp awaiting repatriation to their homeland. Our job was to keep those who wanted to remain in the States confined to the camp. For that purpose, I was appointed as a Sergeant of the Guard with duty scheduled for four hours every third day. A Class A pass was issued, giving me permission to leave the post every time I was off duty but requiring me to be present for reveille every morning.

That seemed rather stupid. What possible purpose could there be for me to get up at 5 a.m. on days when I had no duty, take the bus to camp, stand in line to answer "here" when my name was called, and get back on the bus to go home? I quickly worked out an arrangement with a buddy who lived on the post to answer "here" for me when I wasn't there, and I could sleep in for a continuation of my honeymoon.

One small flaw developed. My buddy went on sick call one day, and there was no one to answer "here" when my name was called. Another friend telephoned me with the bad news that I was AWOL and better get my ass into camp. The MP captain, a non-combat veteran, hated our superior attitude as combat soldiers and gleefully administered company punishment to me. As a result of my one day AWOL, I would be denied Christmas furlough and would have to stand double shifts when most of the guards went home for the holiday. Big deal. My home was where my wife was, at Poor Boy Cabins in Colorado Springs. I willingly put in the required shifts.

The captain was due more irritation. On January 2, 1946, he received orders to present a quota of men for immediate discharge. With the holiday contingent not yet back, he was forced to include me on that list, and orders were cut for me to immediately go to Fort Logan, near Denver, for discharge. Based on the number of points I had accumulated for discharge, my time wouldn't have come up for three more months. Who says crime doesn't pay?

Lois and I packed that night and I grabbed a limo ride to Denver early the following morning. The discharge process was supposed to take two days, so we arranged for Lois to follow me to Denver at the appropriate time, go directly to the railroad station, and await my arrival. Uncle Sam paid for my first-class ticket, but with that money I bought two coach tickets and got us both back to Chicago.

One little hitch almost developed. I had sustained a back injury way back at Camp Swift, and I was still having a problem with backaches. When I mentioned them to the medical officer on discharge, he threatened to hold me over for hospital examination and treatment unless I withdrew my complaint. In the meantime, Lois was sitting in the railroad station waiting for me, with no way for me to contact her. I withdrew the complaint, and we caught the *Rocket* back home. Sitting up in a coach car on the long ride home aggravated my back injury to the point where I needed to seek immediate medical attention.

The day after arriving home, I went to the Veterans' Administration and asked for help. A grizzled veteran of World War I helped me fill out the required paperwork and suggested that I seek private care because it would take months before the VA would establish a service connection to my claim and, until that was done, they would not even give me an examination. It did take months, and the word came down that the VA could not find my medical records despite having the exact dates and place of my hospitalization. Claim denied.

Many years later, my records did surface, but too late. I kept no records of the continuous interim private care, so the VA assumed my back problems were not service connected anyway. Lesson Number One about veterans' care: They'll do anything to avoid spending money on veterans' care when it is needed to support a huge bureaucracy.

THIS WAS THE end of the beginning. With my connection to the military ended, Lois and I began the mundane experience of married life. Lois bore, and we raised, four fine sons who in turn gave us a plethora of grandkids and great-grandkids. It's been a great ride with her for over sixty years.

I guess I did survive for some beneficial reason.

# Epilogue One: Sleepless Nights

On sleepless nights my head still fills with the war.

Shep and Johnny and Ned and the others, in immaculate khaki, wander in and out of my consciousness. In the background, the Italian hills are somewhat familiar.

I look at their faces, always turned partly away or in profile or angled, looking at some distant horizon. I try, but cannot bear to look into their eyes. Nor can they look into mine. We avoid each other's direct, accusative stares.

Is it a sense of guilt because I lived and they died? Are they feeling guilt, too, because they left me to bear the grief alone and in solitude, trying to solve the puzzle?

Shep, at least, left his genes in the world's pool. He had progeny. What gentle nudge did he thus impart to history's course through centuries to come? The youngster he left found me a few years ago, and she found the gentleness to forgive my survival. His generations are still here to make his mark. He was my mentor. A young father figure of indestructibility who nevertheless crumpled in his own blood. Just another victim. His death is still incomprehensible to me. How can a leader die?

I meet for the first time with Jean Mano, the daughter of my dear, departed captain, William M. "Shep" Shepard, in Dallas, December 1998.

(Author photo)

Me (left) with two of my buddies at a reunion in Maine:
Wally Barron and "Fearless" Fosberg

(Author photo)

Johnny and Ned were my friends. We shared everything except, ultimately, life. They left no traceable mark in the chronicles, except perhaps through me.

Knowing that, I try to make a difference for the better. Every day. Perhaps that way, I'll earn a little peace.

General George P. Hays (right) and me at a division reunion in Colorado, shortly before his death in 1978

(Author photo)

Here I am with then-Governor of Texas George W. Bush and 10th Mountain veteran Senator Bob Dole, who was running for president in 1996.

(Author photo)

# Epilogue Two: Postwar Dream

As I rounded the last curve topping Tennessee Pass, Colorado, I could see the figure standing, vaguely familiar, round shouldered and slightly hunched, in the shadow of the red granite marble monument. I wearily opened the car door, stiff and sore from the long drive up through Trinidad, Salida, and Leadville. I got out and stretched a bit before walking up the gravel path to the 10th Mountain Division Memorial which graces the entrance to Cooper Hill/Ski Cooper. As I approached the figure, he turned to me. I recoiled at the realization that it really was Johnny.

In the nearly half century since I had last seen him on Belvedere, he hadn't made it to a single reunion. I hadn't expected to see him here at the 50th Anniversary Reunion, beginning the next day in Vail. We silently embraced with tears running down our cheeks, and ran our fingers down the columns of names identifying the 999 men who never came back. They were all there: Dolan and Shep and Ned and Blais and Craven and all the others whose dreams of the future were shattered by careening bits of steel.

We headed directly up the hill, skirting the woods in which we had bivouacked while in ski school. Faint strains of the harmony we sang wafted through the new growth of pines. We could almost hear the crackling of the campfires as they used to sound when we crawled into down-filled bags for a few hours' sleep to overcome the day's exhaustion. At the end of the tree-lined road, the T-bar tow hut still stood, now accompanied by a pseudo-chalet rather than the skimpy bare-bones mess hall. The T-bar stretched toward the summit at a different angle than the one we remembered, but Chicago Ridge still dominated the skyline. We stood quietly there for a few minutes, then turned and walked slowly back to my car.

Johnny knew he didn't need an invitation as I explained that I was going to re-explore a few of the old mountain roads, and he slid in beside me. Without further conversation, I headed north toward Camp Hale. We paused for a moment at the overlook where photos of the camp had been placed, showing what the now-empty valley once held. At the camp entrance I turned onto the now-crumbling streets, and toward the huge arena-sized rock marking the source of Resolution Creek. The car wheezed a few times but in low gear crawled up the rocky road to where Pearl Creek branched off to the right. Johnny and I exited my car, crossed the rickety aspen bridge, and in a barely remembered mountain-paced walk, climbed to the peak on which we had set up an OP in twenty feet of snow during D Series. Finding no sign of the Camels pack I had discarded after sneaking a smoke under my raincoat, we made our way back to the now-rested automobile.

A few more miles of chugging brought us just under the crest of Ptarmigan, where we had bedded down soaking wet from the Easter Sunday blizzard. It was here that we had stood guard duty in our sleeping bags, linked to each other by strings so we could keep each other awake. We laughed at the thought of our inventiveness, and began the long drive down to Homestake Creek and the rock-climbing area.

The little meadow where we had shared a mountain tent was now overgrown, but it took only a few minutes to find the cliff where Johnny had attempted to climb the overhang, and I had barely held him on the belay when he fell. He nodded silently when I reminded him that he had jokingly cussed me out for letting his glasses break when they fell to the bottom of the cliff. For a while, we perched on a ledge while I reeled off the events of my life since Italy…still married to Lois, whom Johnny knew and remembered…four great sons…and many grandchildren and great-grandchildren whom I adore.

In his usual taciturn manner, Johnny remained silent, just nodding when I gave him the openings in the monologue into which he could thrust the vagaries of the life he had never lived to experience.

We headed toward Vail, and Johnny asked me to drop him off at the information office so he could verify where he was to stay. I headed for my hotel.

I saw neither hide-nor-hair of Johnny until the memorial service several days later. At least I think it was Johnny. What I saw was a shadowy figure standing next to the monument as the eulogy was read for those killed in action, which Henry Moscow had composed for the *Blizzard* in Italy.

Henry was a talented writer who went on to edit the post-war *Life* magazine.

I'll never really be sure it was Johnny. It was hard to tell through all those tears. The tears were pretty much like those I had shed when he died on Belvedere.

## Award of Bronze Star

HEADQUARTERS
10th MOUNTAIN DIVISION
APO #345
U.S. Army

MARTIN L. DANEMAN, 36745423, Corporal, Infantry, United States Army. For meritorious service in combat during the period 20 February 1945, to 10 April 1945, near Mt. Della Torraccia and Mt. Della Spe, Italy. In assisting his battalion adjutant, Corporal DANEMAN rendered valuable and competent service. When his battalion made several moves during an offense, he went forward with the advance party, accomplishing a superior job of guiding and assigning quarters and areas. On reconnaissances and patrols, he proved his courage and ability in entering areas well forward of the lines, and braving sniper fire to seek out routes of advance and positions for battalion installations. On one occasion, when he accompanied the adjutant to a forward observation post and arrived at the height of an enemy counterattack, he voluntarily joined a patrol set out to repulse the enemy, acquitting himself with great bravery and greatly assisting the group in their battle. At all times, his splendid devotion to duty and willingness to assist in every manner possible have earned Corporal DANEMAN the respect and commendation of all. His courage and superior ability are truly worthy of the highest praise. Entered the military service from Chicago, Illinois.

BY COMMAND OF MAJOR GENERAL HAYS
H.F. MILLER
Major, AGD
Asst. Adj. Gen.

Major Miller may have written the very flattering piece above, but the facts he relied on could have come from only one person, Captain William Shepard ("Shep," because you never identified the rank of an officer within earshot of the enemy). Shep was my company commander, and we spent many combat hours together. He was very generous in assessing the value of just doing my job.

The awarding of the Bronze Star medal described above was followed by a second one commonly described as the "Harry Truman" Bronze Star, given in recognition of the Combat Infantry Badge.

# Acknowledgments

I wrote this story to preserve it for my descendants. The story is completely mine, as I remember it. I am responsible for errors in time, place, and fact. I used real names for the most part, but in some instances and for obvious reasons, I made up a few fictitious ones.

I want to thank Audrey K. Wendland for reading my manuscript and giving me encouragement along the way. She is a sister of I-85. Her brother, Lieutenant Keith J. Kvam, was one of the many young officers we lost on that terrible day of April 14, 1945. I never knew him personally, but wish I had. A few years ago, Audrey and I became e-mail friends while working together on a story for the *Blizzard*, the official quarterly publication of the 10th Mountain Division Association. She is an experienced writer and editor and helped turn my hodgepodge of recollections into a readable story.

I also owe a great deal to my granddaughter, Julie Daneman, who spent hours and days reading and correcting the text and translating it into my own vocabulary. Many thanks to Flint Whitlock, co-author of *Soldiers of Skis,* who spent many hours proofreading and improving my original manuscript, and to my publisher, Nan Wisherd, for exercising extreme patience in dealing with my lack of expertise as an author. Endless thanks to my son Phil, whose computer skills leave me dazzled. And to Lois, who continues to be my muse, my inspiration, and the love of my life.

This story is as much theirs as mine.

# Index

**ILLUSTRATIONS: Bold, italics**
**PEOPLE: Bold**